CLAY BAKING
revival of an age-old art

Carmen Bégin

Holt, Rinehart and Winston of Canada, Limited
Toronto — Montreal

CLAY BAKING: REVIVAL OF AN AGE-OLD ART

AUTHOR: Carmen Bégin

COVER: Catie Bégin

INTERIOR: Marie-Josée Bégin

Holt, Rinehart and Winston of Canada, Limited
55 Horner Avenue
Toronto, Ontario
Canada

Printed in Canada
4 5   77 76

ISBN 0-03-929925-2

Library of Congress Card Catalog Number 73-3883

Table of contents

EXAMPLE OF EARTHENWARE

Top right: baker for **meat** or **game** (2 quarts)

Front: baker for cooking **fish** (1½ quarts)

Top left: baker for **red meat** or **game** (3 quarts)

There are also earthenware bakers for **poultry, turkey** (4 quarts or more) and for **chicken** (½ quart).

CURIOSITY, CURIOSITY...?

Curiosity, a virtue dear to women, so they say, sometimes results in a certain heedlessness which leads them "to put their foot in it". In this case, and for a good reason, I put my hand in it plus a little thinking. My "heedlessness" provoked other peoples' curiosity which in turn stimulated mine. This was enough to get me to take a vow of involvement qualified as "noble dilettantism". Like many great adventures, it all started with a chance happening. A potter friend, putting an earthenware pot down on my table, said, "You like cooking, experimenting? Here is a duckbilled platypus; tell me what you can do with it". And indeed, it seemed to me a difficult object to classify with the conventional creatures of my kitchen menagerie.

As I sometimes enjoy working with bizarre utensils or forbidding recipes, I put the apparatus to the test. The discoveries and appreciation which followed were the impetus for new experiences and the enlargement of a repertory that I had difficulty in limiting. Furthermore, I felt the urge to make known, on a small scale, what I had acquired. I was encouraged in this idea by the spontaneous offer of my two daughters to illustrate the proposed book. So, through a mutual challenge, the enterprise became a joint one.

At a time when store shelves are full of newfangled kitchen utensils, bringing out recipes of dishes cooked in earthenware may seem like a paradox. In spite of the many adaptations this noble ancestor of our efficient pots and pans has undergone, in spite of its long journey through civilisation, in spite of its faithfulness in preparing anything from the frugal pittance of hard jaws to the fancy delicacies of dainty palates, how do we explain such a return to the past? Could it be eccentricity, a moral obligation to a prayer from the past, an urge to put old fashioned dishes on the table, thus nostalgically evoking the wonders invented in the good old days?

If that is the case, it would be an accident, for, unfortunately, information about this historic contribution to culinary art does not seem to be available. Perhaps it is the possession of some Sherlock Holmes of the past, or of some historian or anthropologist hoarding, in gray, dusty files, documentation of which they alone know the value.

Lacking ties with the past, I have tried to discover the appropriate methods for our resources and way of life. I have used mainly earthenware or terra cotta made by potters such as Jean Cartier, who has adapted them in form and material to modern production and use.

Carmen Bégin

Practical Advice

1 — ABOUT THE POTS

 The pots, like all clay containers, must be handled carefully. Despite their rather sturdy appearance, they do not resist hard knocks or sudden changes of temperature. Terra cotta pots being porous (absorbent), they retain aromas and surrounding liquids, which the heat releases, and this is why they are known for their aromatic cooking.

2 — ABOUT CUTS OF MEATS, GAME OR FISH

To save time preparing dishes, ask your butcher to cut the meat as indicated in each recipe. Be sure that big pieces will not prevent you from closing the lid tightly.

The amount of time required for preparing the meat recipes does not take into consideration the time that your butcher could save for you, and which could then be subtracted.

As for game and fish, the preparation time is not indicated, for their condition on arrival in the kitchen varies a great deal, depending on whether you have caught them or whether they were bought fresh at a market or frozen.

However, many fishmongers and butchers (in the case of game), agree to prepare them as required. They are generally more accustomed and better equipped, and you can thus save time and avoid the tasks that many consider disagreeable, such as scaling, scraping, filleting fish, etc.

The container must:

- be of porous clay;

- be neither too thin nor too thick;

- have the least possible enamel or obstructions;

- have as water-tight a seal as possible between the two parts;

- have no escape valve for vapor and aroma;

- have an appropriate shape and size for the type of food and quantities to be cooked (poultry, fish, game, stews . . .);

- be easy and safe to handle, especially for putting into and taking out of the oven and for lifting the lid during and after cooking.

After buying, the following procedure is recommended:

- a one-hour bath in hot water (reheated every fifteen minutes);

- this is followed by a vigorous brushing (without soap or detergent) and a simple wiping;

- to dry, place in oven for 10 minutes at 250°F. (dry pot open).

Use

The following procedures can be done simul-taneously, and in this way you can save a great deal of time in preparing the recipes in this book.

- Before putting the ingredients into the pot, im-merse both parts of pot in hot water for 5, 10 or 15 minutes, as indicated in each recipe;

- pre-heat the oven to the required cooking temperature;

- prepare the recipe and put it into the pot;

- do not let the liquid rise above a half-inch under the lip of the lower part;

- be sure that the lid closes properly;

- put it into the oven;

- a few minutes before the time is up, lift the lid and check to see if the food is ready and adjust the amount of time accordingly;

- when it is ready, put it down on a *solid and heatproof* object.

- avoid opening the oven. If you must, do it rapidly but carefully and when necessary take out the pot quickly, closing the oven door to retain the heat.

Cleaning

- Scrape off any remaining food with a smooth object (plastic or rubber spatula, or a wooden spoon);

- immerse in hot water and forget it until the next day or the day after;

- to finish, rub vigorously, preferably with a non-metallic stiff brush (plastic, nylon, etc.) or with pads of rough, absorbent, tough paper, until the ingredients are gone;

- rinse thoroughly with running water and slightly diluted vinegar (this however is not essential);

- dry it open, preferably in the oven for 10 minutes at 250° F.;

- put away, but do not close tightly.

Main causes of damage

- Sudden changes of temperature. Avoid putting a heated pot down on a cold object (wet cloth, heat conducting materials: metal, enamel, porcelain, etc.);

- avoid putting a heated pot on a hot stove burner or warming up food in a cold pot taken for example from the refrigerator. Wait until it is at room temperature before putting it into the oven. (Warmed-up dishes are often better, the aromas having had time to penetrate the ingredients more fully);

- do not put frozen food into the pot, thaw it first;

- handle carefully, avoid hard, angular objects, lift and replace the lid delicately.

Discoloration

- With use, the inside and outside of the pot acquires the color of oak leaves in autumn;

- do not use detergent;

- be delighted, on the contrary, that the pot is showing the signs of a good vintage wine, which improves with age;

- see how your dishes become more flavourful as the discoloration increases.

LAMB

Curried Lamb

INGREDIENTS

2½ pounds lean lamb shoulder, cut in 1 inch cubes
2 medium onions, finely chopped
2 apples, pared, cored and quartered
juice of 1 lemon
1 tablespoon tomato paste diluted in one cup of water
½ cup seedless raisins

SERVINGS
5

PREPARATION
20 minutes

SOAKING TIME OF CLAY BAKER
10 minutes

BAKING TIME
350° F. 1 hour

SEASONINGS
1 tablespoon curry
1 teaspoon ginger
1 pinch cayenne pepper
salt to taste

DIRECTIONS

Lay half the onions on bottom — Add meat, apples — Moisten with lemon juice, tomato paste and water — Add remaining onions — Sprinkle with seasoning — Close and bake — Add raisins twenty minutes before cooking time is up.

SUGGESTED ACCOMPANIMENTS

Steamed rice with paprika or rice pilaf — Vichy carrots or baked bananas — In season, a fresh crisp cucumber salad with shredded fresh mint.

Lamb with Apples

INGREDIENTS

2½ pounds lean lamb shoulder, cut in 1 inch cubes

4 apples, pared, cored and quartered

4 medium onions, chopped

juice of 1 lemon

1 cup broth (beef, chicken or lamb)

SERVINGS
5

PREPARATION
20 minutes

SOAKING TIME OF CLAY BAKER
10 minutes

BAKING TIME
350° F. 1 hour

SEASONINGS
1 teaspoon ginger
1 teaspoon peppermint
salt to taste

DIRECTIONS

Arrange meat cubes in baker — Place apples on top — Cover with onions — Season meat — Moisten with lemon juice and stock — Close and bake.

SUGGESTED ACCOMPANIMENTS

Green kidney beans or curried rice — Green peppers, stuffed with rice — String beans or a simple green salad, using young leaves of dandelions in the spring.

SAUCE : Strain all your baker ingredients — Pour into a saucepan and simmer — Add a small glass of wine or sherry just before bringing it to the table. "Délicieux !"

Crown Roast of Lamb

INGREDIENTS

1 crown roast, with 8 ribs

¼ cup white wine (optional) or juice of 1 lemon

2 tablespoons of capers

SERVINGS

2

PREPARATION

10 minutes

SOAKING TIME OF CLAY BAKER

10 minutes

BAKING TIME

400° F.

¾ hour, well done
½ hour, medium

SEASONINGS

Fresh mint leaves or 1 tablespoon dried mint
salt and pepper to taste

DIRECTIONS

Sprinkle mint leaves on bottom — Add meat, fat side up — Add wine or lemon juice — Close and bake — Dot with capers just before serving.

SUGGESTED ACCOMPANIMENTS

All of the season's fresh vegetables that you can find — Braised endives — Glazed carrots or green peas with asparagus tips — Eggplant salad or watercress salad with lemon dressing.

Lemon Lamb Chops

INGREDIENTS
8 lamb chops, 2 inches thick
1 lemon, peeled and sliced

SERVINGS
4

PREPARATION
10 minutes

SOAKING TIME OF CLAY BAKER
5 minutes

BAKING TIME
400° F.
½ hour (medium)

SEASONINGS
1½ teaspoons cinnamon
1 pinch saffron
pepper

DIRECTIONS
Remove as much fat as possible from the chops — Arrange in row in clay baker — Put a slice of lemon and seasoning on each — Close and bake.

SUGGESTED ACCOMPANIMENTS
Saffron rice or rice pilaf — Artichoke hearts stuffed with spinach — Tomato salad with green string beans or a simple "ratatouille" with steamed rice.

Stuffed Grape Leaves

INGREDIENTS

15 grape leaves
1 pound ground mutton
½ cup cooked rice
1 medium onion, finely chopped
2 eggs, slightly beaten
1 tablespoon of oil
1½ cups broth (mutton, veal
    or chicken)

SERVINGS

4

PREPARATION

35 minutes

SOAKING TIME OF CLAY BAKER

10 minutes

BAKING TIME

300° F. 1 hour

SEASONINGS

1½ teaspoons allspice
salt and pepper to taste

DIRECTIONS

*In a large bowl mix thoroughly: meat. rice. onion. eggs, seasoning —
Rinse grape leaves and wipe dry — On each, put 1 tablespoon meat
mixture — Carefully roll up the leaves — Tie with thread — Oil
bottom of clay baker — Place stuffed leaves in tight rows — Moisten
with broth — Close and bake — Remove thread before serving.*

SUGGESTED ACCOMPANIMENTS

Rice — Leeks with Hollandaise Sauce — Braised tomatoes or
stuffed mushrooms.

NOTE — This dish can be served cold as an hors-d'oeuvre, but then the
rolls should be smaller.

Roast Leg of Mutton

INGREDIENTS

5 pound leg of mutton
  (boned if possible)
2 cloves garlic, halved
3 parsley sprigs
2 tablespoons soya sauce
2 tablespoons dry mustard
4 tablespoons oil
½ lemon, squeezed

SERVINGS
6
PREPARATION
20 minutes
SOAKING TIME OF CLAY BAKER
10 minutes
BAKING TIME
350° F.
1½ hours (medium)
SEASONINGS
1 teaspoon rosemary
1 teaspoon savory
1 teaspoon powdered
  fennel or 4 fresh
  stalks, chopped
salt and pepper to taste

DIRECTIONS

Insert slivers of garlic into the meat — Let stand for 1 hour or more at room temperature — Prepare a paste with soya sauce, oil, mustard, lemon juice — Make a bed of parsley — Place roast on top — Cover roast with paste and seasoning — Close and bake.

SUGGESTED ACCOMPANIMENTS

All the new tender vegetables the season can offer: baby carrots, tiny potatoes, small sweet peas, turnips, beets, etc. — Off-season: red kidney beans or green kidney beans may be appropriate if fresh vegetables are not available — Do not forget a romaine salad with chives and cream dressing — Serve with the traditional mint jelly.

Irish Stew

INGREDIENTS

2 pounds mutton shoulder or leftover roast, cut in fine strips
1 teaspoon of oil
5 medium potatoes, thinly sliced
3 onions, thinly sliced
2 sprigs of parsley, chopped
1 cup lamb broth or other broth (veal, chicken)

SERVINGS
4

PREPARATION
30 minutes

SOAKING TIME OF CLAY BAKER
10 minutes

BAKING TIME
350° F.
1½ hours

SEASONINGS
2 teaspoons savory
2 bay leaves, crushed
salt and a good deal of pepper, which should be the dominant flavour

DIRECTIONS

Oil bottom of clay baker — Alternate layers of potatoes, meat, onions, etc., season each layer until you have used all ingredients — Dot generously with parsley, pepper heavily — Close and bake.

SUGGESTED ACCOMPANIMENTS

Brussels sprouts or French style string beans — Generous chef's salad.

Mutton with Leeks

INGREDIENTS

2½ pounds lean mutton shoulder
cut in small regular cubes
4 small leeks with tops cut
in 2-inch pieces
1 medium onion, chopped
1 cup of water
2 eggs
juice of 1 lemon

SERVINGS
5

PREPARATION
30 minutes

SOAKING TIME OF CLAY BAKER
10 minutes

BAKING TIME
300° F. 1 hour

SEASONINGS
2 teaspoons dry mint
or peppermint
salt to taste

DIRECTIONS

Place leeks, onions, and seasoning in clay baker, finishing with meat — Add mint again — Moisten with water — Close and bake ¾ hour — Remove from oven, being careful of steam when you open lid — Gently fold in the beaten eggs with lemon, using a wooden spoon — Return the uncovered dish to the oven to bake another 15 minutes — Avoid boiling.

SUGGESTED ACCOMPANIMENTS

Boiled parsley potatoes or kidney beans — Lima beans or buttered succotash may be served as well — An escarole salad.

Spring Stew

INGREDIENTS

2 pounds lean boned breast or shoulder of lamb cut in 1 inch cubes
1 tablespoon oil
2 onions, finely chopped
2 cloves garlic, crushed
4 tomatoes (in season), peeled, seeded and mashed, or
   1 cup canned Italian tomatoes, drained
8 new potatoes
4 carrots, peeled and cut in strips
4 turnips, peeled and quartered
1 cup white wine or 1 cup broth (veal or chicken)
juice of 1 lemon
1 package frozen peas

SERVINGS
5 or more

PREPARATION
40 minutes

SOAKING TIME OF CLAY BAKER
10 minutes

BAKING TIME
350° F. 1½ hours

SEASONINGS
1 teaspoon savory
1 tablespoon parsley
1 teaspoon peppermint or crushed mint leaves
salt and pepper to taste

DIRECTIONS

Oil bottom of clay baker — Add meat cubes — Cover with onions, garlic, tomatoes, potatoes, carrots, turnips — Moisten with wine or broth and lemon juice — Sprinkle with seasoning — Close and bake — Twenty minutes before baking is completed, add thawed frozen peas — Finish baking.

SUGGESTED ACCOMPANIMENTS

A green spring salad (dandelion greens with very thinly sliced raw mushrooms, and wild garlic (allium savitum). These may be found wild in moist soil near woody areas. The bulbs are somewhat smaller than the common domestic garlic, but are much sweeter and more tender.

BEEF

Portuguese Steak

INGREDIENTS
4 minute steaks, 1 inch thick
1 teaspoon oil
2 cloves garlic, crushed
¼ cup port or sherry

SERVINGS
4

PREPARATION
10 minutes

SOAKING TIME OF CLAY BAKER
10 minutes

BAKING TIME
350° F.
¾ hour (well done)

SEASONINGS
2 bay leaves, crushed
pinch cayenne pepper on
    each steak
salt to taste

DIRECTIONS
Oil bottom of clay baker — Add steaks — Put garlic and seasoning on each of them — Moisten with port or sherry — Close and bake.

SUGGESTED ACCOMPANIMENTS
Tomatoes or green peppers stuffed with rice — Small carrots — Brussels sprouts with chestnuts — Boston lettuce.

Beef Casserole

INGREDIENTS

2½ pounds beef rump, cut in 1 inch cubes
1 tablespoon oil
4 shallots or 1 onion, minced
2 carrots, sliced
1 celery stalk with leaves, chopped
3 large tomatoes (in season) or 1 can (20 oz.) tomatoes
2 tablespoons cider vinegar
2 tablespoons capers

SERVINGS

4 or more

PREPARATION

20 minutes

SOAKING TIME OF CLAY BAKER

5 minutes

BAKING TIME

350° F. 1 hour

SEASONINGS

2 teaspoons dry mustard
2 bay leaves, crushed
salt and pepper to taste

DIRECTIONS

Oil bottom of clay baker — Arrange cubes — Cover with shallots, carrots, celery and tomatoes — Moisten with vinegar — Season — Close and bake — Five minutes before end of cooking time, dot with capers.

SUGGESTED ACCOMPANIMENTS

Steamed rice — Cauliflower "Polonaise" — Asparagus (in season) or green string beans "à la Française".

Flemish Beef

INGREDIENTS

2½ pounds chuck beef, cut in very thin slices
2 parsley sprigs, chopped
2 cloves garlic, minced
2 medium onions, sliced very thin
1½ tablespoons brown sugar mixed in 1 cup beer

SERVINGS
4

PREPARATION
20 minutes

SOAKING TIME OF CLAY BAKER
10 minutes

BAKING TIME
300° F. 1 hour

SEASONINGS
1 teaspoon thyme
1 teaspoon marjoram
salt and pepper to taste

DIRECTIONS

Sprinkle bottom of clay baker with parsley — Arrange half the meat, onions, remaining meat, garlic — Finish with seasoning — Moisten with beer — Close and bake.

SUGGESTED ACCOMPANIMENTS

Large buttered egg noodles or brown rice, both richly colored with paprika — Broccoli with a dash of lemon juice — A beet salad with anchovies.

Old Fashioned Beef Stew

INGREDIENTS

2½ pounds chuck, round or rump
    beef
2 large onions, chopped
2 cloves garlic, minced
2 celery stalks with leaves, chopped
1 cup white wine or
    1 cup beef broth and
    the juice of 1 lemon
1 tablespoon cognac (optional)

SERVINGS
5

PREPARATION
15 minutes

SOAKING TIME OF CLAY BAKER
10 minutes

BAKING TIME
250° F. 3½ hours

SEASONINGS
2 bay leaves, crushed
1 teaspoon savory
1 teaspoon thyme
4 whole cloves
salt and pepper to taste

DIRECTIONS

Make a bed of half the vegetables and seasoning — Add beef — Cover with remaining vegetables — Add seasoning — Moisten gently, pouring broth or wine and cognac around side of clay baker (do not wash away seasoning, which must remain on top) — Close and bake.

SUGGESTED ACCOMPANIMENTS

Whole small boiled potatoes or large egg noodles — A large romaine salad.

Beef Provençale

INGREDIENTS

2½ pounds bottom chuck or round beef
2 onions, minced
2 carrots, sliced
1 celery stalk with leaves, sliced
12 mushrooms with stems, sliced
1 can (20 oz.) Italian tomatoes, drained and seeded
1 cup rich beef broth
1 orange peel, grated
12 ripe black olives

SERVINGS

5

PREPARATION

20 minutes

SOAKING TIME OF CLAY BAKER

10 minutes

BAKING TIME

350° F. 1½ hours

SEASONINGS

2 teaspoons savory
2 bay leaves, crushed
2 teaspoons marjoram
salt and pepper to taste

DIRECTIONS

Arrange half the vegetables in the baker — Add meat — Cover with remaining vegetables — Sprinkle with grated orange peel — Season — Moisten with broth — Close and bake — Dot with olives ten minutes before serving.

SUGGESTED ACCOMPANIMENTS

Boiled rice or spinach noodles — A generous salad garnished with watercress and cherry tomatoes or beets.

Beef à la Bourguignonne

INGREDIENTS

2½ pounds roundsteak cut in
    2 inch cubes
1 tablespoon oil
4 parsley sprigs, coarsely chopped
2 cloves garlic, crushed
3 carrots, sliced
2 medium onions, chopped
1 pound mushrooms, minced
2 cups Burgundy wine
1 cup beef broth
2 tablespoons tomato paste
2 tablespoons cognac

SERVINGS

5

PREPARATION

30 minutes

SOAKING TIME OF CLAY BAKER

10 minutes

BAKING TIME

300° F. 3 hours

SEASONINGS

2 bay leaves, crushed
2 teaspoons thyme
1 parsley sprig, minced
salt and pepper to taste

DIRECTIONS

Oil bottom of baker — Make bed of parsley — Arrange meat cubes in tight rows — Add vegetables — Season — Moisten with wine and tomato paste diluted in beef broth — Add cognac — Close and bake — After 2 hours of cooking, open baker (be careful of steam), add just enough wine or stock to cover meat — Finish cooking.

SUGGESTED ACCOMPANIMENTS

Boiled potatoes dressed with chopped parsley — Crispy French garlic bread — Spinach with lemon cut "julienne" or green sweet peas — A chef's salad.

Braised Beef

INGREDIENTS
3½ pounds brisket or sirloin beef
3 slices lean salt pork
4 carrots, sliced
2 cloves garlic, crushed
1 orange peel, grated
½ cup water
2 parsley sprigs, minced

SERVINGS
5 or more

PREPARATION
20 minutes

SOAKING TIME OF CLAY BAKER
10 minutes

BAKING TIME
300° F. 2½ hours

SEASONINGS
2 whole cloves
1 teaspoon sage
1 teaspoon savory
salt and pepper to taste

DIRECTIONS
Place pork on bottom — Add beef — Sprinkle top with carrots, onions, garlic and orange peel — Moisten with water — Add seasoning — Close and bake — Just before serving, sprinkle with fresh chopped parsley.

SUGGESTED ACCOMPANIMENTS
Baked or boiled potatoes — Turnips cut "julienne" — Green string beans — Romaine salad with cream dressing.

NOTE — You might wish to make ginger braised beef, by substituting 2 teaspoons fresh grated ginger for whole cloves, and by adding two fresh ripe, peeled, seeded and crushed tomatoes, or off-season, canned Italian tomatoes (half of a 20 oz. can).

Braised Beef Cantonese

INGREDIENTS
1½ pounds round steak, cut in fine strips
1 tablespoons oil
2 cloves garlic, crushed
2 tablespoons finely slivered fresh ginger root *
4 celery stalks, cut in large slivers
2 tablespoons liquid honey diluted in 2 tablespoons water
1/3 cup soya sauce
3 tablespoons sherry

SERVINGS
4 or more

PREPARATION
30 minutes

SOAKING TIME OF CLAY BAKER
10 minutes

BAKING TIME
350° F. 1 hour

DIRECTIONS
Oil bottom of baker — Arrange meat — Add garlic, ginger, and celery — Thoroughly mix honey, water, soya sauce and sherry — Pour over ingredients — Close and bake.

SAUCE: If you want a thicker sauce: pour stock from clay baker into a saucepan — Thicken with 2 tablespoons cornstarch in 4 tablespoons water — Simmer until the sauce is clear — At the end add a little (1 tablespoon) of sherry to enhance the flavour.

SUGGESTED ACCOMPANIMENTS

Steamed or fried rice — Lotus root or cucumber salad with fresh mint, or an exotic salad made of mandarin oranges, grapefruit sections, chinese lettuce and watercress.

* Ginger roots are available in Oriental and Caribbean food markets or in specialty food shops. If dry ginger is used, which is far less tasty, remember that one teaspoon dry ginger equals one tablespoon fresh.

Beef with Onion Sauce

INGREDIENTS

3 beef shanks, cut in pieces
  2 inches thick or
  2½ pounds round, rump or chuck
    beef cut in cubes 2 inches thick
1 tablespoon oil
1 package dehydrated onion soup
½ cup water

SERVINGS

4 or more

PREPARATION

10 minutes

SOAKING TIME OF CLAY BAKER

10 minutes

BAKING TIME

250° F. 4 hours

SEASONINGS

fresh parsley sprigs or
  fresh chervil in season

DIRECTIONS

Oil bottom of clay baker — Add meat — Spread dehydrated soup evenly on top — Moisten with water — Close and bake — Just before serving, sprinkle generously with minced parsley or chervil.

SUGGESTED ACCOMPANIMENTS

Large egg noodles or small boiled potatoes — Raw spinach salad with tomatoes — Baby carrots in season; or all the abundant fresh summer vegetables you can find.

NOTE — If you want to ignore the clock, this recipe and many others might prove to be of some help. Just lower the oven temperature to 200° F. and continue to bake for several hours. Do not forget that baking in clay bakers elminates shrinkage, basting and turning.

Corned Beef

3½ to 4 pounds beef brisket or boned rump
2 cloves garlic, slivered
1 onion, chopped
2 carrots, sliced
2 celery stalks, sliced
1 orange, peeled and sliced
1 cup water

SERVINGS
6

PREPARATION
15 minutes

SOAKING TIME OF CLAY BAKER
10 minutes

BAKING TIME
250° F. 4 hours

SEASONINGS
2 tablespoons pickling spices
white pepper to taste

DIRECTIONS

Wash meat well with wet cloth — Let it soak in cold water 2 hours (change water once or twice); you may need to soak it longer, depending on the degree of salinity of your meat. Supermarket meat is generally less salty than what your butcher may offer you. Ask his advice on the curing process — Slash meat in several places — Insert slivers of garlic — On the bottom place the onions, carrots and celery — Add meat — Put orange slices on top — Moisten with water — Close and bake.

SUGGESTED ACCOMPANIMENTS

Boiled potatoes, turnips and carrots or boiled cabbage with green string beans.

Cabbage Rolls

INGREDIENTS
1 medium cabbage
1 pound ground beef or pork
1 cup cooked rice
3 shallots with tops, finely cut
1 parsley sprig, chopped fine
1 egg, slightly beaten
1 tablespoon oil
1 can (10 oz.) stewed tomatoes
  or in season, 3 large ripe tomatoes;
  peeled, seeded and mashed

SERVINGS
5 or more
PREPARATION
35 minutes
SOAKING TIME OF CLAY BAKER
10 minutes
BAKING TIME
300° F. 2 hours
SEASONINGS
1 teaspoon allspice
1 teaspoon sage
1 teaspoon thyme
salt and pepper to taste

DIRECTIONS
Remove cabbage stump — Simmer cabbage in salted water for 10 minutes — Remove from heat and place under cold running water for a minute — Dispose of the outer leaves — Detach twelve leaves, cut off the white, hard stems, spread on a towel to dry. Mix: beef or pork, rice, shallots, parsley, egg, seasoning, blending with wet hands to obtain homogeneous mixture — Put 1 tablespoon or more of mixture on each leaf — Fold up on three sides to form a rectangle — Tie with string — Oil bottom of clay baker — Place shredded cabbage leaves on bottom — Arrange cabbage rolls in line — Moisten with soup and tomatoes — Season again to taste — Close and bake.

SUGGESTED ACCOMPANIMENTS
Boiled rice with the rich tomato sauce taken from the clay baker — French style green string beans or yellow beans make a good combination.

Chuck Wagon Stew

INGREDIENTS

2½ pounds bottom round or chuck
   beef, cut in 2 inch cubes
1 tablespoon oil
4 medium potatoes, diced
4 carrots, diced
4 apples, pared, cored and sliced
1 onion, minced

SERVINGS
5

PREPARATION
30 minutes

SOAKING TIME OF CLAY BAKER
10 minutes

BAKING TIME
300° F. 2½ hours

SEASONINGS
2 teaspoons parsley
2 bay leaves, crushed
2 teaspoons thyme
salt and pepper to taste

DIRECTIONS

Oil bottom of baker — Arrange layer of meat — Season — Add layers of potatoes, carrots, and apples, until you have used all the ingredients, finishing with the meat and onions — Season — Close and bake.

SUGGESTED ACCOMPANIMENTS

A coleslaw salad goes well with this economical dinner. Do not forget the traditional hot and crispy homemade bread.

This simple family dish is a favourite in Saskatchewan.

Stewed Heart of Beef

INGREDIENTS
1 beef heart, 3 to 3½ pounds
½ pound salt pork, sliced very thin
2 cups dry red wine
1 cup wine vinegar (for the marinade)
2 large onions, chopped
2 cloves garlic, minced
15 mushrooms, sliced

SERVINGS
4 or more

PREPARATION
35 minutes

SOAKING TIME OF CLAY BAKER
10 minutes

BAKING TIME
250° F.   3 hours

SEASONINGS
2 teaspoons thyme
4 bay leaves
4 whole cloves
pepper to taste

DIRECTIONS
Cut heart in half lengthwise — Let stand in cold water for one hour — Meticulously remove nerves and clogged blood — Wash thoroughly — Wipe dry — Cut into small pieces — Marinate 6 hours in shallow pyrex pan with vinegar, 1 onion, 4 cloves, 1 clove garlic, bouquet garni, salt and pepper — Drain well — Place salt pork in bottom of baker — Add pieces of marinated heart — Cover with remaining onions, garlic and mushrooms — Season again — Add red wine — Close and bake.

SUGGESTED ACCOMPANIMENTS
Mashed potatoes — Carrots — Spinach with grated lemon peels or a simple iceberg lettuce salad.

Andalusian Steak

INGREDIENTS

5 tenderloin steaks, cut 1 inch thick
1 tablespoon oil
4 shallots, finely chopped
1 small eggplant, peeled and
   finely diced
2 sweet green peppers, finely diced
1 can (20 oz.) tomatoes or, in season
   3 large ripe tomatoes peeled,
   seeded and mashed

SERVINGS
5

PREPARATION
20 minutes

**SOAKING TIME OF
CLAY BAKER**
5 minutes

BAKING TIME
400° F. ½ hour, or less,
   if desired medium rare

SEASONINGS
1 teaspoon cardamom
2 teaspoons rosemary
chives or fresh parsley to
garnish

DIRECTIONS

Oil bottom of baker — Add steaks — Cover with shallots, eggplant and peppers — Season — Close and bake 20 minutes — Remove lid (beware of steam), cover steaks with tomatoes, bake another 10 minutes uncovered. Sprinkle with chives or parsley before bringing it to the table.

SUGGESTED ACCOMPANIMENTS

Saffron rice or fluffy mashed potatoes — Fried julienne potatoes are also successful — Stuffed mushrooms or artichoke hearts filled with spinach au gratin make a more elegant combination — To complete, an endive salad or canned palm hearts en vinaigrette. "Savoureux!"

Dutch Hodgepodge

INGREDIENTS

2 pounds of flank, plate or brisket beef
4 carrots, diced
2 onions, finely chopped
4 potatoes, diced
2 cups (or more) water
1 tablespoon butter
2 tablespoons milk

SERVINGS

5

PREPARATION

20 minutes

SOAKING TIME OF CLAY BAKER

10 minutes

BAKING TIME

300° F. 2 hours

SEASONINGS

chives and parsley,
coarsely chopped
salt and pepper to taste

DIRECTIONS

Arrange successive layers of meat, carrots, onions, potatoes, etc. — Season each layer — Barely cover with water — Close and bake one hour — Remove clay baker from oven (beware of steam) — Remove meat, cut in very fine pieces — Make a purée of the vegetables, adding milk and butter — Place meat on top — Sprinkle with herbs — Close and finish baking.

SUGGESTED ACCOMPANIMENTS

A generous raw vegetable salad. Children like this simple dish.

Braised Beef Tongue

INGREDIENTS

1 fresh beef tongue (about 3 or 4 pounds)

4 slices lean salt pork

1 veal shank, 1 inch thick, cut crosswise

1 large onion, chopped

4 carrots, sliced

2 cloves garlic, crushed

1 cup dry white wine or 1 cup dry cider

½ cup beef broth

SERVINGS
4 or more

PREPARATION
1 hour

SOAKING TIME OF CLAY BAKER
10 minutes

BAKING TIME
250° F. 4 hours

SEASONINGS
1 teaspoon basil

2 teaspoons coriander seeds

4 whole cloves

1 bay leaf

1 teaspoon peppermint

1 teaspoon parsley

1 teaspoon rosemary

1 teaspoon thyme

salt and pepper to taste

DIRECTIONS

Soak tongue in cold water for approximately six hours — Simmer, for two hours, in a covered kettle of salted water — Remove tongue, plunge for a minute in cold water — Peel off skin — Lay sliced salt pork in bottom of baker — Make a bed of onions, carrots and garlic — Add tongue — Arrange pieces of veal shank around it — Spread seasoning evenly — Moisten with wine or cider and beef stock — Add salt and pepper — Close and bake.

SAUCE: Strain juice out of the clay baker into a saucepan — Add raisins and pine nuts if desired — Thicken the sauce with cornstarch (2 tablespoons in half-cup of water) — A small glass of Madeira wine (2 tablespoons) as a final touch makes it an elegant dish.

NOTE — May also be served cold: sliced, garnished with watercress, radishes and cherry tomatoes, it becomes a good buffet table dish.

Meat Loaf

INGREDIENTS

1 pound ground beef or pork
1 cup cooked rice
4 shallots with tops, minced
2 celery stalks, finely cut
1 small sweet green pepper,
  finely diced
1 clove garlic, crushed
1 egg, lightly beaten
2 tablespoons cognac or dry sherry
  and juice of 1 lemon
10 green olives stuffed with red
  sweet pepper
1 tablespoon oil
1 can (20 oz.) stewed tomatoes or
  tomato soup

SERVINGS

6 or more

PREPARATION

35 minutes

SOAKING TIME OF CLAY BAKER

15 minutes

BAKING TIME

300° F. 1¾ hours

SEASONINGS

2 teaspoons allspice
2 teaspoons sage
salt and pepper to taste

DIRECTIONS

Blend with wet hands: beef, rice, shallots, celery, pepper, garlic, egg and seasoning — Deposit mixture on waxed paper — Form an oblong-shaped loaf (press well on all sides) — At regular intervals, insert olives into loaf — Cover with tomatoes — Close and bake.

SUGGESTED ACCOMPANIMENTS

Brown rice, fried rice or mashed potatoes — Celeriac salad or coleslaw. May be served cold on a buffet table.

GAME

Note

It is preferable to cook game or fish in a pot kept for that purpose. The strong flavour of game, for example, seeps into the clay, and leaves its mark on other foods. Guard jealously the bakers that you set aside for game or fish; your extra attention will be rewarded by the pure flavours which will result.

Many birds and wild game need to be marinated before cooking, either to tenderize the meat or to flavour it. A general marinade is suggested on page 52. You need not be a slave to it. Adapt it to your taste by using your favourite spices.

The quantity of the marinade is not indicated, nor the preparation time. The quantity depends upon the amount and type of game, and the size of the baker. The length of time you marinate the meat depends on its condition when you get it: either freshly killed and still whole, or killed earlier and cut in smaller pieces.

The marinade can be made in your clay-baker or in a glass bowl (avoid metal) and placed in a cool spot, away from the light. Turn the meat several times. If the marinade is cooked it will permeate the food rapidly. If it is uncooked, it will take longer.

Marinade

AROMATIC BASE:

Approximately 1 onion, 2 shallots, 1 carrot, 2 celery stalks, 1 or 2 garlic cloves, thyme, bay leaf, parsley, whole pepper, 2 cloves, to which can be added either a few coriander seeds, juniper, rosemary, basil, marjoram, orange or lemon peel, nutmeg, cinnamon, etc. Add these aromatic substances to the liquid, whose quantity will vary according to the size of the piece of meat to be marinated.

LIQUID:

2 or 3 tablespoons of oil, ¼ cup of wine vinegar (or more for the big pieces of meat), 2 or 3 cups of dry white wine or red wine (white wine, being lighter, will accentuate the taste of the meat; red wine being heavier, will make the sauce richer), then a little water, and some cognac.

PREPARATION: Cooked Marinade

Cook the aromatic substances in the oil — moisten with wine and vinegar and let it simmer for ¼ hour to ½ hour. Allow it to cool before pouring it on the meat.

Uncooked Marinade

Surround the meat to be marinated with the aromatic substances, sprinkle it with oil and cover with liquid.

Turn the piece of meat over several times while it is steeping. Before cooking, drain it and wipe it with a cloth or absorbent paper.

My Own Quail Recipe

INGREDIENTS
4 quails
4 or more grape leaves
½ pound bacon
2 tablespoons sherry
juice of ½ lemon

SERVINGS
2 or 4

SOAKING TIME OF CLAY BAKER
15 minutes

BAKING TIME
300° F.   45 minutes

SEASONINGS
sage
salt and pepper to taste

DIRECTIONS

Allow for one or two quails per person — Stuff birds as indicated below, or make a stuffing of your own with either fruit or bread — This will provide a few more bites to eat, since the birds are so small — Wash and wipe the quails dry — Rub with lemon juice — Season on inside and outside — Sprinkle interior with sage — Put in as much stuffing as possible — Truss — Wrap each bird in one or more grape leaves — Wrap the bundle again with bacon strips — Tie with string — Place on bottom of clay baker — Moisten with sherry — Close and bake.

STUFFING: Giblets, minced — ¼ cup wild or yellow rice well cooked — 4 finely cut dry prunes, soaked in sherry — 1 ounce blanched nuts cut fine — 1 shallot with tops minced — 1 egg lightly beaten — 1 tablespoon sherry — 1 teaspoon melted butter — Mix all ingredients thoroughly, using hands to obtain homogeneous mixture.

NOTE — The same stuffing may be used for grouse or squab. Allow ⅓ cup for each bird; the mixture will expand as it cooks, so do not pack it firmly. Leftover stuffing may be wrapped in grape leaves and cooked with the birds.

SUGGESTED ACCOMPANIMENTS

If used as an entrée, serve on toast, garnished with watercress or fiddlehead greens — For a more nourishing dish, serve with pilaf rice, carrots and sweet peas or asparagus tips (in season).

Duck à l'Orange

INGREDIENTS

1 domestic duck (4 to 5 pounds)
1 orange, quartered
1 small onion, quartered
1 apple, quartered
1 celery stalk with leaves,
   chopped
1 clove garlic, minced
1 tablespoon sugar
juice of 1 orange
juice of ½ lemon
4 parsley sprigs
½ cup cider (or apple juice)
1 orange, peeled (for garnishing)
2 tablespoons of orange liqueur
   (for the sauce)

SERVINGS

4

SOAKING TIME OF CLAY BAKER

10 minutes

BAKING. TIME

300° F. 2 hours

SEASONINGS

1 teaspoon curry powder
1 teaspoon cumin
salt and pepper to taste

DIRECTIONS

Clean duck and wipe dry — Season cavity generously with salt and pepper — Place inside duck: orange, onion, apple, celery, garlic, sugar, orange and lemon juice — Lay bird on bed of parsley and celery leaves — Moisten with juices — Sprinkle with curry and cumin — Close and bake.

SAUCE: When duck is done, set aside on a hot platter — Discard parsley and celery leaves — Spoon fat out of baker — Pour the good stock in a saucepan, simmer (do not boil) — Add the orange liqueur — Taste, and if necessary, add pepper or lemon juice — For a milder sauce, add one tablespoon of currant jelly. Before serving, put the duck back into the clay baker, decorate breast with orange slices — Serve hot sauce separately.

NOTE — Allow at least 1 pound of duck per person — Duck is difficult to carve — Cut in quarters and serve each person a quarter.

SUGGESTED ACCOMPANIMENTS

Wild rice or yellow rice with mushrooms — Small peas and small onions — Turnips are also excellent. For salad: endives with grapefruit and mandarin sections topped with sour cream or a plain watercress and lemon salad.

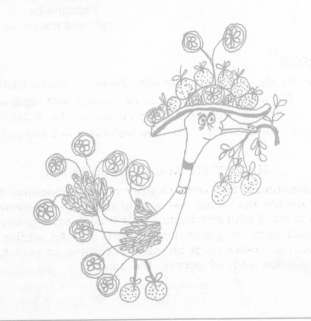

Baie-Jolie Wild Duck with Apples

INGREDIENTS

2 ducks
6 apples; pared, seeded and quartered
½ lemon
4 slices salt pork
2 tablespoons sugar or maple syrup
1 large onion, minced
¼ cup cider (or apple juice)

SERVINGS

5 or more

SOAKING TIME OF CLAY BAKER

10 minutes

BAKING TIME

300° F. 2 hours

SEASONINGS

1 teaspoon marjoram
1 teaspoon cinnamon
(optional)
salt and pepper to taste

DIRECTIONS

Wash and dry ducks well — Rub with lemon — Season interior and exterior — Put four apple quarters in each cavity with sugar or syrup — Truss — Place lard and onions on bottom of clay baker — Add birds — Dot with seasoning — Moisten with cider — Close and bake.

SUGGESTED ACCOMPANIMENTS

If you have guests and want to offer a more spectular dinner, you may double the recipe, serve wild rice with mushrooms — Brussels sprouts with chestnuts — Or French style green beans with grilled nuts or grated lemon peels — An endive salad with fruit. The choice must be made according to your budget, your inspiration and, of course, the season.

Caribou du Père Yvon

INGREDIENTS

1 piece saddle of caribou, about
   5 pounds, marinated 2 days in
   white wine
¼ pound bacon
1 onion, minced

SERVINGS

5 or more

**SOAKING TIME OF
CLAY BAKER**

10 minutes

BAKING TIME

400° F. 1 - 1½ hours,
   well-done

SEASONINGS

parsley leaves
celery leaves
salt and pepper to taste

DIRECTIONS

*Make a bed of parsley and celery leaves — Put half the onions in the
baker — Add meat — Arrange bacon strips on top with remaining
onions — Season — Close and bake.*

SUGGESTED ACCOMPANIMENTS

Boiled or mashed potatoes — Cauliflower "polonaise" — Green
peas — Canned palm hearts — Salad with thin slices of uncooked mushrooms — Currant jelly served separately.

NOTE — This recipe can also be used for moose.

Moose Stew

INGREDIENTS

3 pounds moose, cut in 2-inch cubes, marinated in dry red wine 6 to 12 hours
¼ pound bacon
2 large carrots, sliced
2 onions, minced
1 clove garlic, crushed
2 cups wine from the marinade
2 tablespoons cognac

SERVINGS
5

SOAKING TIME OF CLAY BAKER
10 minutes

BAKING TIME
300° F. 2 hours

SEASONINGS
1 teaspoon thyme
2 parsley sprigs
1 teaspoon marjoram
chives
salt and pepper to taste

DIRECTIONS

Place bacon on bottom of baker — Add meat with carrots, onions and garlic — Moisten with strained marinade and cognac — Close and bake — Dot with fresh chives before serving.

SUGGESTED ACCOMPANIMENTS

Potatoes Lyonnaise or boiled parslied potatoes — Escarole salad or red cabbage salad.

NOTE — Roe-deer may be cooked the same way, but six hours is sufficient marinating time. The meat cut is not given here, as usually the meat is a gift from a hunter. If it is a tender part, do not stew it. Roast it as in "Caribou du Père Yvon", and marinate only six hours. If you are lucky enough to have a resident hunter and your own freezer, you will find among these recipes sufficient information to cook any cut of meat.

Jugged Hare

INGREDIENTS
1 hare cut in pieces, marinated in white wine 12 hours
4 slices bacon
1 large onion, minced
1 clove garlic, crushed
12 mushrooms, minced
1½ cups marinade, strained
1 cup water
juice of ½ lemon

SERVINGS
5

SOAKING TIME OF CLAY BAKER
10 minutes

BAKING TIME
300° F. 3 hours

SEASONINGS
1 parsley sprig
1 teaspoon savory
1 teaspoon marjoram
salt and pepper to taste

DIRECTIONS
Put bacon and onions in baker — Arrange pieces of meat — Add garlic — Season — Sprinkle mushrooms moistened with lemon juice — Pour liquids over all — Close and bake.

SUGGESTED ACCOMPANIMENTS
Small parslied potatoes — Braised parsnips — Sweet peas or New Brunswick fiddlehead greens — Cucumber and yoghurt salad.

NOTE — Rabbit may be cooked in the same way.

Pheasant with Cream Sauce

INGREDIENTS
1 pheasant
¼ pound bacon
2 tablespoons sherry

STUFFING:
2 shallots, sliced
2 tablespoons butter
pheasant's liver, chopped
¼ pound ground lean pork

SAUCE:
½ cup cream
juice of 1 lemon
2 tablespoons sherry
1 egg yolk

SERVINGS
4

SOAKING TIME OF CLAY BAKER
10 minutes

BAKING TIME
350° F. 1½ hours

SEASONINGS
1 teaspoon sage
1 teaspoon marjoram
2 parsley sprigs
salt and pepper to taste
paprika

DIRECTIONS

In a pan, melt butter, add shallots and liver and sautée about ten minutes — Mix this well with the ground pork and the seasoning — Stuff mixture in cavity of bird — Truss — Wrap bacon strips around it — Put pheasant on bed of parsley — Moisten with sherry — Sprinkle with salt, pepper and paprika — Close and bake.

SAUCE: Remove pheasant from clay baker, place on a hot platter — Strain the sauce into a saucepan and simmer — Remove pan from heat — Beat well: sherry, lemon juice, cream and egg yolk and pour over pheasant.

SUGGESTED ACCOMPANIMENTS
Big mushrooms, stuffed and grilled — Wild or yellow rice — Green string beans or fiddlehead greens — A salad of lettuce with fruit and avocado.

Hare with Prunes and Chestnuts

INGREDIENTS

1 hare (5 to 6 pounds) cut in pieces, marinated in red wine
4 thin slices salt pork or 4 strips bacon
1 onion, chopped
2 carrots, sliced
2 cups wine from the marinade, strained
1 cup water
18 dried prunes soaked in tea or sherry
1 can unsweetened chestnuts or 1 pound blanched chestnuts *
1 tablespoon cognac or brandy

SERVINGS
6

SOAKING TIME OF CLAY BAKER
10 minutes

BAKING TIME
250° F. 3 hours

SEASONINGS
1 teaspoon rosemary
1 teaspoon thyme
salt and pepper to taste

DIRECTIONS

Cover bottom of baker with layers of pork or bacon slices, onions and carrots — Add pieces of hare — Moisten with wine and water — Season — Close and bake 2½ hours — Remove clay baker from oven, arrange prunes and chestnuts around pieces of hare — Close and bake another ½ hour — Add cognac to the sauce just before serving.

SUGGESTED ACCOMPANIMENTS

Boiled parslied potatoes — Salsify fried in batter — Fresh spinach salad with lemon julienne and tomatoes.

* To blanch chestnuts (to remove shell), cut a ½″ gash across the flat side of each nut with a sharp vegetable knife — Cover with water and slowly bring to a boil — Remove nuts from the shells — Cover with boiling water, let stand for six minutes and drain.

Wild Goose Bécancour

INGREDIENTS

1 wild goose cut in pieces and marinated (turn many times) in white wine for two days (in refrigerator) *
4 thin slices salt pork
2 onions, minced
5 apples, pared and minced
2 cloves garlic, minced
1 cup apple juice or cider
1 cup marinade, strained
capers (about 2 tablespoons)

SERVINGS
5 or 6

SOAKING TIME OF CLAY BAKER
10 minutes

BAKING TIME
250° F. 4 hours

SEASONINGS
1 parsley sprig, chopped
2 teaspoons marjoram
2 bay leaves
salt and pepper to taste

DIRECTIONS

Place salt pork, onions, apples and garlic in baker — Add pieces of bird — Dot with herbs, season — Pour apple juice or cider and marinade — Close and bake — Before serving, sprinkle with capers.

SUGGESTED ACCOMPANIMENTS

Baked beans New York style, lentils or baked or mashed potatoes, unless you can afford wild rice — Braised endives or fennel — Tomato salad or a more elaborate chef's salad.

* This wild goose, called "outarde" in French, is far bigger than the wild Long Island ducklings or those from Eastern Canada. The "outarde" weighs as much as six pounds, is somewhat tougher and needs to be marinated and cooked much longer.

Partridge with Cabbage

INGREDIENTS
2 partridges
1 small cabbage
4 thin slices salt pork
1 carrot, scraped
1 onion, chopped
1 clove garlic, crushed
1 cup water
1/4 cup dry white wine
1/4 cup port

SERVINGS
2 or 4

SOAKING TIME OF CLAY BAKER
10 minutes

BAKING TIME
250° F. 3 hours

SEASONINGS
2 teaspoons savory
2 teaspoons dry parsley or 1 fresh sprig, chopped
salt and pepper to taste

DIRECTIONS

Plunge cabbage into salted boiling water — Remove the outside leaves — Shred cabbage — Place pork and cabbage in bottom of clay baker — Season well — Add carrots, onions, and garlic — Nestle birds into the mixure — Season again — Moisten with water, wine and port — Close and bake.

SUGGESTED ACCOMPANIMENTS

Small boiled potatoes dotted with butter and garnished with finely chopped parsley — Carrots — Or a salad of red beans with chopped green pepper, en vinaigrette.

Lake Dumont Partridge

INGREDIENTS
2 partridges
6 or more grape or cabbage
   leaves
¼ pound bacon
2 parsley sprigs
juice of 1 lemon
2 tablespoons white vermouth
2 tablespoons apple juice or cider

SERVINGS
4

SOAKING TIME OF CLAY BAKER
10 minutes

BAKING TIME
300° F. 2 hours

SEASONINGS
1 teaspoon sage
salt and pepper to taste

DIRECTIONS

Clean bird, wipe dry and rub with lemon — Season interior and exterior with sage, salt and pepper — Wrap each partridge in 1, 2 or 3 grape leaves (depending on size of each bird) — Wrap bacon around — Tie with thread or string — Lay parsley in bottom of clay baker — Place bird — Moisten — Close and bake.

SUGGESTED ACCOMPANIMENTS
Sweet potatoes or butternut squash — Braised Turnips — Green string beans — Red cabbage salad.

Roast Buffalo

INGREDIENTS
4 pounds boned buffalo roast
(choice tender meat)
4 strips bacon
5 parsley sprigs
1 onion, minced
1 tablespoon cognac

SERVINGS
6 or more

SOAKING TIME OF CLAY BAKER
5 minutes

BAKING TIME
400° F. 1½ hour
(more for well done)

SEASONINGS
steak spices to taste

DIRECTIONS
*Make a bed of parsley and half the onions in baker — Add roast —
Place bacon and remaining onions on roast — Season — Close and
bake.*

SUGGESTED ACCOMPANIMENTS

Baked potatoes with sour cream and chives or creamed mashed
potatoes — Braised fennel or cauliflower "polonaise" — Sweet
green peas with asparagus tips — Boston lettuce with mandarin
oranges and grapefruit sections, if your dessert does not consist
of fruit. A dish of currant jelly may be a welcome accom-
paniment.

NOTE — Buffalo meat has become available due to the overpopulation of the
buffalo herds in the Elk Island National Park in Alberta, Canada. The meat is
exported to many parts of America. Buffalo meat is very lean and the cuts
are similar to beef, but it is important to slice across the grain; otherwise
the meat would be tough and stringy. There are many ways of cooking it. The
meat may be marinated if a special flavour is desired or if you wish to mask
the gamey flavour of the buffalo itself. For additional cooking tips see recipes
for: Beef à la Bourguignonne; Braised beef; Beef Casserole.

Squab Stew with Raisins

INGREDIENTS
4 squabs*, cut in two
giblets chopped
3 bacon strips
1 onion, chopped
1 cup Muscat raisins
1 cup white wine
1 parsley sprig
1 teaspoon thyme
2 bay leaves
salt and pepper to taste

SERVINGS
4

SOAKING TIME OF CLAY BAKER
10 minutes

BAKING TIME
300° F. 1½ hours

DIRECTIONS
Place bacon, giblets, onion, in bottom of baker — Add squabs — Sprinkle with seasoning — Moisten with wine — Close and bake — 10 minutes before end of cooking, add raisins — Close again and finish baking.

SUGGESTED ACCOMPANIMENTS
Wild rice or fluffy mashed potatoes — Sweet green peas — Small beets with a generous sprinkling of fresh herbs — Raw scraped carrots in salad en vinaigrette.

* Squabs or baby pigeons, usually weigh one pound; they are considered one of the finest delicacies. If you serve them as a party food, the suggested accompaniments for Pheasant in Cream Sauce would make excellent fare.

FISH
&
SHELLFISH

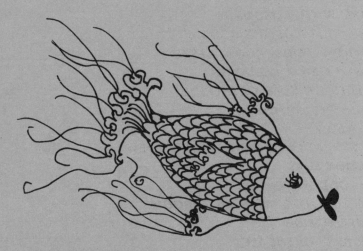

Note

Meat, fish and game should be cooked in their own bakers. Since the porous clay tends to retain the flavours, they will not disappear even with a good brushing in vinegar or running water, and will accentuate the taste of later dishes.

The cost of another baker is certainly justified if you eat much fish, a protein which is usually cheaper than meat. The cost of the bakers should not keep you from cooking in earthenware. They are well worth the price because of the fact that they retain all the natural flavours and nutritional value of the food.

The cooking method is very simple, and is based on general recipes to which you can add your own personal touch. The titles of the following recipes refer to a particular fish, shell-fish or mollusc. But with each one there is a list of others (obtainable fresh or from a market) which can be easily substituted.

Saguenay Periwinkles

INGREDIENTS
4 dozen periwinkles in their shells
1 onion, quartered, studded with cloves
2 cups water
sea salt (if available) or a generous quantity of salt and pepper

SERVINGS
4

SOAKING TIME OF CLAY BAKER
10 minutes

BAKING TIME
500° F. 15 minutes

SUBSTITUTES
clams, crab, crayfish, mussels, prawns, scampi, shrimps, squid, etc.

DIRECTIONS
Wash periwinkles meticulously in a lot of water — Drain well — Put onions and seasoning in baker — Add periwinkles and water — Close and bake — Allow more time to bake if you choose scampis or any bigger shellfish.

SUGGESTED ACCOMPANIMENTS
Served as an hors-d'œuvre, periwinkles are taken out of their spiral shells with an oyster fork or nutpick and dipped in a hot butter-and-garlic sauce which also contains lemon juice and fresh chopped parsley.

NOTE — These molluscs are sold in retail markets. They rarely measure more than 1"-1½" in diameter. If you have the chance to gather them yourself, by the sea, select the largest from the crowded colonies. Do not confuse these periwinkles with the French, Swiss, Italian or Japanese snails, which are much bigger and are sold in cans.

Uncle Omer's Chowder

INGREDIENTS

3 pounds smelts, thoroughly cleaned
4 potatoes, thinly sliced
4 onions, sliced
2 tablespoons butter
chopped parsley and celery leaves
salt and pepper to taste
2 cups water

SERVINGS

4

SOAKING TIME OF CLAY BAKER

5 minutes

BAKING TIME

300° F. 1½ hours

SUBSTITUTES

cod, halibut, croaker, haddock, etc. All non-oily fish

DIRECTIONS

Put successive layers in the baker: potatoes, onions, fish, butter, greens and seasoning — Barely cover with water — Close and bake.

NOTE -- "Bouillotte" is a type of chowder that is a great favourite in the Eastern Quebec townships, where, in winter, smelts are caught under the ice and tossed outside to freeze near the fishing huts. After eating the potage of the "kettle of fish", one can partake of excellent fried smelts or "poulamon" (small cod), which are so tasty that one's appetite is boundless.

Clam Chowder

INGREDIENTS

2 dozen fresh clams, in juice or
  1 can clams with juice (20 oz.)
2 medium-sized potatoes, finely diced
4 shallots with greens, minced
2 celery stalks, finely diced
2 cups clam juice (add water to
  obtain 2 cups)
1½ cups warm milk
½ cup heavy cream
1½ tablespoons fresh, or
  1 tablespoon dry, minced parsley
4 pinches saffron
salt and pepper to taste

SERVINGS
4

SOAKING TIME OF CLAY BAKER
5 minutes

BAKING TIME
300° F. 30 minutes;
200° F. another
  20 minutes

SUBSTITUTES
canned: crab, lobster,
  tuna, (without oil)
fresh: oysters, mussels,
  scallops, shrimps,
  prawns; chopped

DIRECTIONS

Place in bottom of baker: potatoes, shallots, celery, herbs, seasoning — Pour liquid over it — Dot with butter — Close and bake half an hour at 300° F. — Lower oven temperature to 200° F. — Add warm milk and clams or a substitute of your choice — Close and bake another 20 minutes — Remove from oven and, according to taste, sprinkle with fresh parsley and toasted bread cubes — Add a dot of butter in each soup bowl just before bringing it to the table — Check seasoning.

Carp Alsacienne

INGREDIENTS
1 3-pound carp, completely cleaned
½ lemon
3 cups sauerkraut
1 tablespoon butter
½ cup white wine or chicken broth
1 dozen oysters (if available)
salt and pepper to taste
Mornay sauce *

SERVINGS
4

SOAKING TIME OF CLAY BAKER
15 minutes

BAKING TIME
400° F. ¾ hour

SUBSTITUTES
whole fresh lean fish:
  cod, mullet,
  muskellunge, pickerel,
  pike, sole, etc.

DIRECTIONS
Rub fish with lemon after cleaning it with wet cloth — Season on all sides — Put sauerkraut well loosened in baker first — Bury carp in it — Dot with butter — Moisten with wine — Close and bake — Remove from clay baker (beware of steam), fold in Mornay sauce with oysters — Place under grill without lid long enough for the edges of the oysters to begin to curl.

* **MORNAY SAUCE:** 2 tablespoons butter — 2 tablespoons flour — 2 cups milk — 4 tablespoons grated gruyère cheese — 1 egg — 4 tablespoons cream — Salt and pepper. Let butter melt in saucepan — Add flour, stir with wooden spoon, moisten with warm milk, season — In a bowl, mix eggs and cream — Fold into sauce a little at a time, stirring constantly — Sprinkle with grated cheese — Stir until smooth, do not boil (medium heat only throughout).

SUGGESTED ACCOMPANIMENTS
Boiled small potatoes — Carrots or sweet potatoes — Or else, peas or asparagus tips.

Shrimps in Whisky

INGREDIENTS
2 pounds fresh shrimps (6 or 8 per person)

MARINADE
2 tablespoons oil
2 tablespoons soya sauce
¼ cup whisky
juice of one lemon
¼ cup dry cider or apple juice
3 tablespoons liquid honey
4 slices fresh ginger or
    2 teaspoons powdered ginger
black pepper to taste

SERVINGS
4

SOAKING TIME OF CLAY BAKER
5 minutes

BAKING TIME
500° F. 15 minutes

SUBSTITUTES
prawns, scampi, lobster

DIRECTIONS
Thaw shrimps if frozen — Peel raw — Remove dark vein from center back — Wipe with damp cloth — Pour marinade in a flat-bottomed glass pan — Let shrimps marinate one hour in refrigerator, turning them once to allow marinade to penetrate entirely — Lay shrimps in rows in clay baker — Moisten with marinade — Close and bake — Garnish with watercress before bringing to the table.

SUGGESTED ACCOMPANIMENTS
Serve as an hors-d'œuvre on a bed of lettuce with watercress and lemon. Serve as a main dish on a bed of rice mixed with blanched slivered almonds and raisins. The sauce may be served piping hot in a separate dish, to moisten the rice. A chef's salad goes well with this dish.

Salmon Steaks

INGREDIENTS

2½ pounds fresh salmon steak
   1½'' thick
1 tablespoon oil
1 carrot, grated
2 shallots, minced
1 lemon, thinly sliced
2 tablespoons white vermouth
2 tablespoons cider or apple juice
   with juice of ½ lemon
salt and pepper to taste

SERVINGS
4

SOAKING TIME OF CLAY BAKER
10 minutes

BAKING TIME
475° F. 25 minutes

SUBSTITUTES
pike, sturgeon, flounder, cod, kingfish, shad, swordfish, tuna, doré, trout.

DIRECTIONS

Wipe fish clean with damp cloth — Rub it with lemon, salt and pepper on both sides — Oil bottom of clay baker — Add: carrot, shallots, lemon — Arrange steaks — Moisten — Close and bake.

SUGGESTED ACCOMPANIMENTS

New spring potatoes — In season, baby carrots — Green string beans, tied together to form one portion for each person — Sweet fresh peas, etc. — Coleslaw seasoned with fresh herbs according to season and inspiration: chervil, basil, chives, parsley, poppy or sesame seeds, tarragon, mint. Off-season, if you can find zucchini, make a salad of it slightly boiled and thinly sliced, Italian style; this is delicious chilled. Combine it with string beans or artichokes en vinaigrette.

Doré with Almonds

INGREDIENTS
1 whole doré ,(3½ pounds)
thoroughly cleaned
2 carrots, grated
2 parsley sprigs
4 shallots
1 lemon, sliced
2 bay leaves, crushed
6 fennel leaves, crushed
salt and pepper to taste
½ cup dry white wine or cider
2 oz. blanched, peeled, slivered
almonds, toasted in 2 tablespoons
butter

SERVINGS
4 or more

SOAKING TIME OF CLAY BAKER
5 minutes

BAKING TIME
450° F. 40 minutes

SUBSTITUTES
cod, pike, bass, flounder,
pollock, pickerel, sole,
etc.

DIRECTIONS

Place in bottom of baker: carrots, parsley, lemon — Wipe fish clean with damp cloth — Rub with lemon, salt and pepper on all sides — Put shallots inside the fish — Place fish in baker — Sprinkle bay and fennel on top — Moisten — Close and bake — Just before serving, decorate fish with almonds sauteed in hot butter.

SUGGESTED ACCOMPANIMENTS

As an hors-d'œuvre : bring the clay baker to the table and serve as is, with abundant sauce and hot homemade bread. As a main dish: serve with rice or julienne fried potatoes — Spinach or green string beans, unless you can find fiddlehead greens sold in frozen packages. In season, asparagus is the ideal green vegetable.

Escargots de Bourgogne

INGREDIENTS
1 can (4½ oz.) large snails (24)
1 lemon, thinly sliced
4 shallots, minced
4 cloves garlic, crushed
4 tablespoons parsley, minced
¼ pound butter
salt and pepper

SERVINGS
4

SOAKING TIME OF CLAY BAKER
5 minutes

BAKING TIME
500° F. 10 minutes

DIRECTIONS

Wash snails in a strainer under running cold water — Drain well — Arrange in bottom of baker: lemon, shallots, snails — Add garlic, parsley and dot of butter on each of them — Season — Close and bake. Serve on small earthenware plate kept hot in the oven; serve six snails per person, cover with plentiful sauce taken from the clay baker, with one lemon slice per person. Also, you may serve them on triangular toast garnished with watercress and lemon.

NOTE — This type of cooking avoids the exacting process of inserting the snails in a shell. What's more, the distinct flavour is enhanced by exposing the snails completely to the seasonings in the clay baker. The same preparation is well adapted to: lobsters, prawns, crabs, oysters, mussels, clams and frog legs. The baking time will vary according to weight.

Snails in Mushroom Nests

INGREDIENTS

24 large mushroom caps
1 lemon, squeezed
24 large snails, without shells
   (in can, 4½ oz.)
1 lemon, thinly sliced
2 cloves garlic, minced
4 tablespoons fresh or dry
   parsley, chopped very fine
¼ pound butter
salt and fresh-ground pepper

SERVINGS

4

SOAKING TIME OF CLAY BAKER

5 minutes

BAKING TIME

500° F. 15 minutes

DIRECTIONS

Remove mushroom stems (reserve for soup) — Wash and dry caps, sprinkle them with a touch of lemon — Season on all sides — Arrange mushrooms top side down in bottom of clay baker — Insert snail in each cap — Sprinkle with minced garlic and parsley — Dot with butter — Season again — Close and bake — Serve on triangular toasted pieces of bread — Decorate with watercress and lemon slices taken from the clay baker.

NOTE — This recipe was inspired by the French chef Curnonsky's "escargots en friche", in which indigenous mushrooms and wild garlic are used. In Eastern Canada, and New England states, both garlic and mushrooms may be found abundantly in nearby woods. The large variety could inspire a new recipe every day.

Baked Fish à l'Orange

INGREDIENTS

2 pounds fish fillets, preferably white-fleshed
1 tablespoon butter
rind of 1 orange, grated
juice of 1 orange, squeezed
2 tablespoons basil
fresh-ground pepper to taste

SERVINGS

4

SOAKING TIME OF CLAY BAKER

5 minutes

BAKING TIME

450° F. 20 minutes or more, according to thickness of fillets

SUBSTITUTES

bluefish, cod, flounder, haddock, kingfish, shad, etc.

DIRECTIONS

Wipe fish with damp cloth — Put butter on bottom of clay baker — Add fish — Sprinkle with orange juice — Season — Sprinkle orange rind — Close and bake.

SUGGESTED ACCOMPANIMENTS

Fresh early vegetables if you have your own vegetable garden — Rice, lentils, noodles in the winter; serve your family's favourite. Do not forget a green vegetable: asparagus, broccoli, string beans, spinach, etc.

Fillets of Sole Catherine

INGREDIENTS
2½ pounds fillet of sole
½ lemon
2 shallots with greens, minced
2 fennel leaves, chopped
salt and pepper to taste
White sauce *
½ cup Malaga grapes, peeled
  and seeded
½ cup dry white wine or cider

SERVINGS
4

SOAKING TIME OF CLAY BAKER
5 minutes

BAKING TIME
450° F. 25 minutes

SUBSTITUTES
bass, cod, flounder, etc.

DIRECTIONS
Wipe fillets clean — Rub with lemon, salt and pepper on all sides — Place in clay baker — Cover with shallots, fennel — Moisten with wine or cider — Close and bake.

* **WHITE SAUCE**: See Mornay Sauce described in Carp Alsacienne, omitting the gruyère cheese. You may vary a white sauce to your liking and give your fish a new, intriguing taste by using: capers, anchovies, lemoned mushrooms, tomato paste (1 tablespoon), horseradish (1 tablespoon) , half-cup pureed spinach, blanched almonds, finely minced red and green peppers, etc. Any of these suggestions will change the taste and appearance of your dish.

SUGGESTED ACCOMPANIMENTS
Steamed rice — Cauliflower, broccoli, asparagus (in season), or cucumbers with fresh mint and cream in summer.

Mackerel Creole

INGREDIENTS

4 fresh mackerel (about 3 pounds)

1 lemon

4 ripe tomatoes; peeled, seeded and
   mashed, in summer, or
   1 can Italian tomatoes (20 oz.)
   without seeds and juice

1 leek, chopped

½ sweet green pepper, finely diced

½ sweet red pepper, finely diced

pinch of saffron

paprika

salt and pepper to taste

SERVINGS

4

**SOAKING TIME OF
CLAY BAKER**

10 minutes

BAKING TIME

400° F. ½ hour

SUBSTITUTES

herring or any fish of the
   season

DIRECTIONS

*Eviscerate, remove head, clean and wipe fish — Rub with lemon, salt
and pepper on all sides — Arrange successive layers of tomatoes, leek,
peppers — Add fish — Finish with a dash of lemon, a pinch of saffron,
and paprika — Close and bake.*

SUGGESTED ACCOMPANIMENTS

**Steamed or fried rice — Cauliflower — Sweet peas — A green
salad.**

Stewed Eel

INGREDIENTS

3 pounds of eel, cut in pieces
   3 inches long
1 medium onion, minced
2 potatoes, finely diced
¼ cup uncooked rice
2 cups or more boiling water
1 parsley sprig, chopped
1 teaspoon savory
salt and pepper to taste

SERVINGS
4

SOAKING TIME OF CLAY BAKER
5 minutes

BAKING TIME
300° F. 1½ hours

DIRECTIONS

Try to buy eel thoroughly cleaned; if not, remove skin, let stand 15 minutes in a quart of cold salted water — Wipe dry — Rub with lemon, salt and pepper — Cut eel into fine fillets — Discard back bone — Put layers of vegetables in baker first, then fish, and seasoning — Submerge in boiling water — Close and bake.

SUGGESTED ACCOMPANIMENTS

Serve with hot garlic French bread, or whole wheat bread, oven-crisp — Generous raw vegetable salad.

Newfoundland Fisherman's Stew

INGREDIENTS
2 pounds fresh cod, diced
2 potatoes, finely diced
2 leeks, chopped
celery leaves, chopped fine
1 slice lean salt pork
boiling water to cover vegetables
2 cups hot milk
salt and pepper

SERVINGS
4 or more

SOAKING TIME OF CLAY BAKER
5 minutes

BAKING TIME
350° F. 30 minutes
250° F. another
    20 minutes

SUBSTITUTES
all fish (non-oily)

DIRECTIONS
Put successive layers of potatoes, leeks, celery greens, seasoning and pork in clay baker — Cover with boiling water — Close and bake ½ hour — Remove clay baker from oven (be careful of steam), lower oven temperature — Add pieces of fish — Stir in hot milk — Season again — Close and bake another 20 minutes.

SUGGESTED ACCOMPANIMENTS
Serve with toast or a loaf of homemade bread.

NOTE — This simple stew is often made by fishermen right on the fishing wharves. They cook it in a large iron kettle, but by using clay, the flavour and attractiveness of the dish is enhanced.

Salmon Loaf

INGREDIENTS

1½ cups bread crumbs
½ cup milk
2 eggs, lightly beaten
1 cup cottage cheese
4 shallots with greens, finely chopped
1 can (16 oz.) salmon
½ lemon, pressed
3 tablespoons fresh parsley, chopped
3 hard-boiled eggs
salt and pepper to taste
paprika
1 tablespoon vegetable oil
8 thinly sliced rings of sweet red or green peppers

SERVINGS
5 or more

SOAKING TIME OF CLAY BAKER
10 minutes

BAKING TIME
350° F. 1 hour

SUBSTITUTES
canned: crab, lobster, sea scallops, tuna; finely chopped

DIRECTIONS

In a large bowl mix in order: bread soaked in milk and squeezed dry, eggs, cheese, shallots, flaked salmon (discard backbone), parsley, lemon juice, seasoning — Knead with wet hands to obtain homogeneous mixture — Oil bottom of clay baker — Add ⅓ of mixture — Place peeled, hard-boiled eggs (boiled 10 minutes) end to end — Add remaining mixture to form an oval-shaped loaf — Press with hands — Sprinkle generously with paprika — Decorate with ring of red or green sweet peppers — Close and bake — Ten minutes before end of baking time, remove dish — Encircle the loaf with buttered sweet peas.

NOTE — A coat of raw red or green sweet peppers finely chopped may be placed on top of the loaf instead of cooked rings; this will add vivid colour and taste.

Seafood Pâté

INGREDIENTS

1 pound fillet of sole

½ pound each clams, oysters, shrimps or prawns, and scallops

salt and pepper with a pinch of allspice

½ cup Madeira wine or dry sherry

juice of ½ lemon

4 tablespoons butter

2 cups cream-puff paste *

4 hard-boiled eggs

SERVINGS

6 or more

SOAKING TIME OF CLAY BAKER

5 minutes

BAKING TIME

300° F. 2 hours

DIRECTIONS

Wipe fish with damp cloth — Sprinkle with lemon — Marinate two hours in Madeira or sherry (use a flat glass dish to ensure equal distribution of marinade in fish) — Turn fish over twice — Season — In another dish, flake the shellfish (you may use a meat grinder) — Mix them with cream-puff paste — Start your dish by placing half the shellfish mixture in the clay baker — Add fish fillets — Line up hard-boiled eggs, end to end — Cover with remaining mixture — Moisten with marinade — Close and bake.

---

* **CREAM-PUFF PASTE:** 1 cup water — ½ pound butter — 1 teaspoon salt — 1 cup flour — 3 eggs. Heat water, salt and butter in a heavy-bottomed 2-quart saucepan; bring to a boil — Remove from heat and immediately pour in all the flour at once; beat with a wooden spoon to blend thoroughly — Set back over moderate heat and beat again with a wooden spoon for a minute or two, until mixture leaves sides of pan and spoon clean, and

creates a film on bottom of pan — Remove from heat — Let cool ten minutes — Break one egg into the center, beat vigorously — Repeat for the remaining eggs, beating until thoroughly absorbed, and paste is smooth.

NOTE — This pâté may be served cold and is an attractive addition to a buffet dinner.

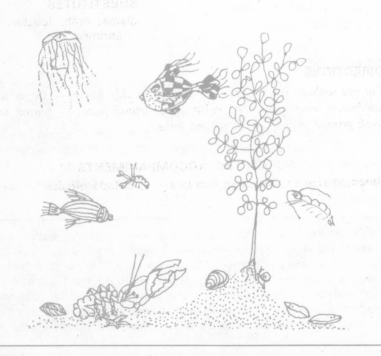

Sea Scallops with Mushrooms

INGREDIENTS

1 pound sea scallops
1 can (10 oz.) cream of
   mushrooms, minced
10 mushrooms, minced
½ lemon, pressed
pepper to taste

SERVINGS
4

SOAKING TIME OF CLAY BAKER
10 minutes

BAKING TIME
350° F. 30 minutes

SUBSTITUTES
clams, crab, lobster,
   shrimps, etc.

DIRECTIONS

Cut sea scallops in even pieces — Place in clay baker — Cover with mushroom soup and sliced mushrooms, lemon juice — Season with fresh ground pepper — Close and bake.

SUGGESTED ACCOMPANIMENTS
Steamed rice or large egg noodles — "Salade niçoise".

Stuffed Fish

INGREDIENTS

1 2½ pound sea trout

½ lemon

3 tablespoons fine breadcrumbs moistened with milk and squeezed dry

2 egg yolks

2 tablespoons butter

1 shallot, finely chopped

½ cup dry white wine or cider

salt and pepper to taste

SERVINGS
4

SOAKING TIME OF CLAY BAKER
10 minutes

BAKING TIME
400° F. 30 minutes

SUBSTITUTES
grey lake trout, bluefish, snapper, bass, red mull, etc.

DIRECTIONS

If you are not lucky enough to have your fish cleaned and boned at your fish market, you may easily do it yourself with a little care and practice. Split the fish down the back from just above the dorsal fin to the tail and remove the backbone by pulling gently, prying with the tip of your knife to avoid waste — Wipe fish clean — Never wash with water — Rub with lemon, salt and pepper inside and outside — Blend stuffing with hands: breadcrumbs, butter, shallots, egg yolks — Stuff fish — Sew opening closed or use skewers held in place by string — Place fish in clay baker — Moisten with wine or cider — Close and bake.

SUGGESTED ACCOMPANIMENTS

Steamed rice or noodles — Spinach braised in cream — Cherry tomatoes cooked with zucchini or eggplants "à la provençale". The season, budget, guests or family are your best guide.

Squid Provençale

INGREDIENTS

2 pounds squid
2 tablespoons oil
2 onions, minced
1 clove garlic, minced
4 large tomatoes, peeled,
   seeded and mashed, or
   1 can (20 oz.) Italian tomatoes,
   without juice
¼ cup dry white wine
¼ cup water
2 bay leaves, crushed
4 parsley sprigs, chopped

SERVINGS

4

SOAKING TIME OF CLAY BAKER

5 minutes

BAKING TIME

300° F. 1 hour

DIRECTIONS

Clean thoroughly in cold water, removing eyes, tentacles, mouth — Let stand 2 hours in cold salted water — Drain and pat dry — Cut squids in small pieces — Blanch in boiling water for 5 minutes — Drain again — Oil bottom of clay baker — Add onions, squids, garlic and tomatoes — Moisten — Sprinkle with herbs and save some fresh parsley for the end, to garnish — Close and bake — Sprinkle with parsley before bringing it to the table — May be served hot or cold.

SUGGESTED ACCOMPANIMENTS

Boiled rice or saffron rice — Green salad with plenty of water-cress sprinkled with lemon, or Madame Irene B. Hoffman's Spring Salad: young dandelion leaves, young sorrel, nasturtium, tarragon, burnet, upland cress, oil, vinegar and chives.

Rolled Fillets of Sole Lucie

INGREDIENTS
2 pounds fillet of sole
1 large carrot, grated
4 shallots with greens, minced
1 lemon, thinly sliced
1 tube of anchovy paste (2 oz.)
2 tablespoons capers
¼ cup white wine
½ lemon, pressed
celery greens, chopped
2 bay leaves, crushed
2 parsley sprigs, chopped
salt and pepper

SERVINGS
4 or more

SOAKING TIME OF CLAY BAKER
5 minutes

BAKING TIME
450° F. 25 minutes

DIRECTIONS
Wipe fillets with damp cloth — Cut them to obtain similar sizes if possible — Lay one by one on a piece of waxed paper, sprinkle each of them with lemon, salt and pepper — Spread anchovy paste evenly (approximately 1 teaspoon on each) — Roll fillet, fix with toothpick — Place on bottom of clay baker: carrots, shallots, herbs, and lemon slices — Line up fish rolls — Moisten with wine and lemon juice again — Close and bake — Before serving, remove toothpicks — Put 3 or 4 capers on top of each roll.

SUGGESTED ACCOMPANIMENTS
As an entrée, serve with triangular whole wheat toast. As a family main dish, serve with fried or boiled rice — Asparagus or broccoli, unless you are able to find the New Brunswick fiddlehead greens, sold frozen.

PORK

Glazed Bacon

INGREDIENTS
3½ pounds back bacon

PASTE:

1 cup brown sugar
1 tablespoon dry mustard
2 tablespoons oil
2 teaspoons ginger
2 teaspoons cardamom or
   ½ teaspoon cayenne pepper

SERVINGS
5

PREPARATION
15 minutes

SOAKING TIME OF CLAY BAKER
15 minutes

BAKING TIME
350° F. 1½ hours

SEASONINGS
parsley or
   chervil (in season)
watercress to garnish

DIRECTIONS

Place meat in baker — Pat paste on top of bacon — Close and bake — Before serving, garnish heavily with parsley or chervil and decorate with a crown of watercress.

SAUCE: Pour sauce in a saucepan — Skim off excess fat — Add a touch of brandy or dry vermouth — Simmer but do not boil — Thicken with 1 tablespoon of cornstarch in ½ cup water — Cook on a low flame until sauce is clear — Add a touch of brandy or dry vermouth — Pour over bacon or serve separately in the saucepan.

SUGGESTED ACCOMPANIMENTS

Hard-boiled eggs quartered, sprinkled with paprika and arranged on watercress — Green beans, brussels sprouts with chestnuts, or a red cabbage salad with coriander seeds and peeled, raw apples.

Pork Chops with Apples

INGREDIENTS

8 pork chops, well-trimmed
2 tablespoons oil
2 tablespoons soya sauce
1 tablespoon liquid honey
2 cloves garlic, crushed
2 apples, pared, cored and sliced

SERVINGS
4

PREPARATION
15 minutes

SOAKING TIME OF CLAY BAKER
10 minutes

BAKING TIME
350° F. 1 hour

SEASONINGS
cinnamon (on apples to taste)
salt and pepper

DIRECTIONS

In a jar, put: oil, soya sauce, honey and garlic — Close tightly and shake vigorously — Pour on bottom of clay baker — Line up chops — Season — Close and bake for ¾ hour — Remove clay baker (be careful of steam) and rapidly arrange apple slices, sprinkled with cinnamon, over meat — Close again and cook another 15 minutes — In season, when using cooking apples, which are firmer, cook an additional 15 minutes.

SUGGESTED ACCOMPANIMENTS

Steamed or fried rice — Belgian endives or braised leeks — Carrots with a generous sprinkling of parsley or a Spanish salad.

Épaule de porc Viennoise
Pork Shoulder Viennese

INGREDIENTS

3½ pounds pork shoulder, boned, rolled and well-trimmed

2 cloves garlic, cut into slivers

¼ pound salt pork

2½ pounds sauerkraut (available canned)

2 onions, studded with four whole cloves

1 cup beer

SERVINGS
6

PREPARATION
20 minutes

SOAKING TIME OF CLAY BAKER
15 minutes

BAKING TIME
300° F. 3½ hours

SEASONINGS
2 bay leaves
10 juniper berries
6 peppercorns
salt and pepper to taste

DIRECTIONS

Insert slivers of garlic between the fat and the meat of the pork at room temperature — Put slices of salt pork in baker — Add half the sauerkraut — Place pork on that bed — Cover with remaining sauerkraut — Season — Place an onion at each end — Moisten with beer — Close and bake.

SUGGESTED ACCOMPANIMENTS

Boiled potatoes — Hot apple sauce — Hot crispy bread — And cold beer as the Viennese serve it, if you like it.

Pineapple Ham

INGREDIENTS
3½ pounds ham shoulder, rolled or picnic or cottage roll, pre-cooked

1 large onion, minced

½ cup pineapple juice

2 tablespoons gin or dry sherry

juice of ½ lemon

pineapple slices to garnish

SERVINGS
6

PREPARATION
15 minutes

SOAKING TIME OF CLAY BAKER
10 minutes

BAKING TIME
350° F. 1 hour, if pre-cooked
250° F. 2½ hours, if raw

SEASONINGS
1 tablespoon dry mustard
8 whole cloves
1 teaspoon cinnamon on pineapple (to taste)
1 teaspoon ginger

DIRECTIONS
Cut off plastic wrapping on ham — If unwrapped and raw, you may have to parboil ham to remove salt — Rub with juice and sherry or gin — Close and bake — Ten minutes before serving, decorate with pineapple slices sprinkled with cinnamon or ginger, or both if you like — A garnish of red and green cherries adds gaiety to your dish — Close and bake another ten minutes or more (time to heat the fruit).

SUGGESTED ACCOMPANIMENTS
Hard-boiled quartered eggs garnished with minced chives or parsley — Whipped potatoes — A green vegetable like: spinach, asparagus, or broccoli, according to the season.

Loin Pork Roast

INGREDIENTS

4 pounds boned tenderloin of pork
2 cloves garlic, slivered
4 parsley sprigs
1 large carrot, scraped
2 onions, minced
4 stalks of celery
¼ cup dry white wine
juice of ½ lemon
4 tart apples, pared, cored
and quartered

SERVINGS

6

PREPARATION

20 minutes

SOAKING TIME OF CLAY BAKER

10 minutes

BAKING TIME

300° F. 2½ hours

SEASONINGS

1 tablespoon dry mustard
1 teaspoon rosemary
1 teaspoon sage
salt and pepper to taste
cinnamon on apple (to taste)

DIRECTIONS

Carefully remove all excess fat — Insert slivers of garlic into meat and rub with mustard, herbs and seasoning — Put parsley, carrots, half the onions, celery into baker — Add meat — Cover with remaining minced onions — Moisten with wine and lemon juice — Close and bake — One-half hour before end of cooking time, crown roast with apples sprinkled with cinnamon — Close and finish baking

SUGGESTED ACCOMPANIMENTS

Lentils or mashed potatoes — Fresh spinach salad with lemon — Or red cabbage "à la flamande".

Ham Slices with Prunes

INGREDIENTS
4 slices ham 1½ inches thick
2 parsley sprigs
4 celery stalks with leaves
2 tablespoons brown sugar
juice of 1 lemon
12 pitted prunes soaked in tea
   until swollen

SERVINGS
4

PREPARATION
15 minutes

**SOAKING TIME OF
CLAY BAKER**
10 minutes

BAKING TIME
350° F. ¾ hour

SEASONINGS
2 teaspoons cinnamon
   or powdered cloves

DIRECTIONS
Put parsley and celery on bottom of baker — Cover with ham slices sugared and seasoned with cinnamon or cloves — Moisten with lemon juice — Close and bake half-hour — Remove clay baker (beware of steam) and place prunes attractively around ham — Close and finish baking another 15 minutes.

SUGGESTED ACCOMPANIMENTS
Red kidney beans or marrow squash or the same vegetables suggested to accompany Pineapple Ham.

POULTRY

Rock Cornish Hen

INGREDIENTS
1 or 2 hens
giblets chopped fine
½ lemon
1 teaspoon oil
4 shallots, chopped
2 parsley sprigs
2 tablespoons sherry

SERVINGS
2 or 4

PREPARATION
15 minutes

SOAKING TIME OF CLAY BAKER
5 minutes

BAKING TIME
350° F. 1 hour

SEASONINGS
1 teaspoon sage
1 tablespoon parsley
salt and pepper to taste

DIRECTIONS
Clean hens meticulously and wipe dry — Rub with lemon half, salt and pepper — Stuff birds: giblets, shallots, sage, parsley, salt and pepper — Truss — Oil bottom of clay baker — Make a bed of parsley — Add birds — Moisten with sherry — Close and bake.

SAUCE: Pour stock into a saucepan. Add 2 tablespoons of cognac (or the juice of ½ lemon), 1 tablespoon currant jelly, a pinch of Cayenne pepper. Heat without boiling (about 4 minutes). Serve separately in a sauce dish.

SUGGESTED ACCOMPANIMENTS
Wild rice or saffron rice — Glazed onions studded with one clove each — Small buttered carrots — Artichoke hearts "en vinaigrette'.

NOTE — A great variety of stuffings may add a little zest to this dish: bread or fruit (apples, apricots, prunes, raisins with wild or plain rice), chestnut, celery or meat and chestnut stuffing.

Tarragon Chicken Breasts

INGREDIENTS
4 half breasts of chicken
1 or 2 carrots, grated
4 shallots with greens, chopped
2 parsley sprigs, chopped
½ cup white wine
1 tablespoon cognac (optional)

SERVINGS
5

PREPARATION
20 minutes

SOAKING TIME OF CLAY BAKER
10 minutes

BAKING TIME
300° F. 1½ hours

SEASONINGS
1 tablespoon tarragon
(fresh tarragon is so
much better, if you ha-
ve it in your garden.)
salt and pepper

DIRECTIONS
Season breasts on all sides — Put on bottom of clay baker: grated carrots, shallots and parsley — Arrange breasts in a tight row (skin on top) — Moisten with wine and cognac — Season and sprinkle with tarragon — Close and bake.

SAUCE: Pour liquid from clay baker, strain — Heat slightly in a saucepan — Add ½ cup heavy cream, an egg yolk, a pinch of tarragon — Heat a minute or two — Serve in a separate sauce dish.

SUGGESTED ACCOMPANIMENTS
Steamed rice with mushrooms crowned with a stuffing of your own or a "mousse de foie gras" makes it a dish for a special occasion.

Cartier Baked Chicken

INGREDIENTS
1 chicken, 4½ pounds
2 parsley sprigs
2 onions, quartered
1 clove garlic, minced
1 celery stalk with leaves, chopped
juice of 1 lemon
½ cup dry white wine

SERVINGS
4 or more

PREPARATION
20 minutes

SOAKING TIME OF CLAY BAKER
10 minutes

BAKING TIME
350° F. 2 hours

SEASONINGS
1 teaspoon rosemary
paprika
salt and pepper to taste
1 teaspoon basil

DIRECTIONS
Clean the chicken carefully — Rub it inside and outside with lemon, herbs and seasoning — Insert onions and garlic in cavity — Put celery, celery leaves and parsley on bottom of clay baker — Add bird — Moisten with wine — Close and bake.

SUGGESTED ACCOMPANIMENTS
Baked potatoes or fried rice — Egg noodles.

NOTE — If the colour of your chicken (or any other meat or fish with white flesh) has not turned a pleasing golden shade, return the uncovered clay baker to the oven under the grill for a few minutes. You may otherwise sprinkle with paprika or any other fresh herbs of the season (chervil, chives, parsley); very finely chopped green and red peppers enhance both taste and appearance.

Chicken with Soya Sauce and Honey

INGREDIENTS
4 chicken legs, cut in half
2 chicken breasts, cut in half

MARINADE
2 tablespoons vegetable oil
¼ cup soya sauce
¼ cup liquid honey
¼ cup white wine (or cider)
juice of 1 lemon
¼ cup fruit juice (pineapple, peach, pear, etc.)
4 fresh ginger roots, grated
3 cloves garlic, crushed
white pepper to taste

SERVINGS
5 or more

PREPARATION
20 minutes

SOAKING TIME OF CLAY BAKER
10 minutes

BAKING TIME
400° F. 1 hour

DIRECTIONS
Put the marinade in a jar with a tight-fitting lid — Shake vigorously — Lay the chicken in a flat pyrex plate — Pour marinade over and let stand (turning occasionally) in the refrigerator for 4 hours — Put meat in clay baker with marinade — Close and bake.

SUGGESTED ACCOMPANIMENTS
Steamed rice served with the tasty and plentiful sauce from the chicken — A handful of pine nuts or blanched nuts, or green or black olives will complement this dish — Broccoli.

Capon Stuffed with Fruit

INGREDIENTS
1 5 pound capon
2 fresh parsley sprigs
2 celery stalks with leaves
2 tablespoons sherry
juice of 1 lemon

STUFFING
1 cup diced toasted bread, moistened
   with milk and squeezed dry
1 celery stalk, finely diced
2 shallots with greens, finely chopped
6 dry prunes, cut in small pieces
6 dry apricots, cut in small pieces
½ can (14 oz.) chestnuts, cut in half
2 small apples; pared, cored and diced
1 handful (about 3 oz.) blanched
   white nuts, split
1 egg, lightly beaten
2 tablespoons sherry
1 tablespoon melted butter
2 bay leaves, crushed
2 teaspoons sage
salt and pepper to taste

SERVINGS
5

PREPARATION
45 minutes

**SOAKING TIME OF
CLAY BAKER**
10 minutes

BAKING TIME
350° F. 2½ hours

SEASONINGS
2 bay leaves
2 teaspoons sage
salt and pepper to taste

DIRECTIONS

Clean, dry, rub capon with seasoning — Prepare stuffing in a large bowl, using wet hands to blend the ingredients — Stuff cavity — Truss meticulously — Make a bed of parsley and celery on bottom of clay baker — Place bird on it — Moisten with sherry and lemon juice — Close and bake.

SUGGESTED ACCOMPANIMENTS

**For a real feast: wild rice or fried rice with mushrooms —
Grilled tomatoes — Tiny French peas — Or a salad of thin
slices of uncooked mushrooms.**

Curried Chicken

INGREDIENTS

8 pieces of chicken (about 4 pounds)
1 tablespoon vegetable oil
1 large onion, chopped
2 large apples; pared, cored and diced
1 can (10 oz.) mushrooms, sliced
½ cup cider (or apple juice)
2 tablespoons sherry
juice of 1 lemon
crushed nuts
hard-boiled eggs, ground or Muscat raisins

SERVINGS
5 or more

PREPARATION
20 minutes

SOAKING TIME OF CLAY BAKER
10 minutes

BAKING TIME
350° F. 1½ hours

SEASONINGS
2 teaspoons curry
1 teaspoon turmeric
1 teaspoon powdered ginger
pinch of saffron
pinch of cardamom
salt to taste

DIRECTIONS

Oil bottom of baker — Add pieces of chicken — Cover with onions, apples, mushrooms — Mix seasoning well in cider — Pour on top of chicken — Close and bake — Before serving, dot with crushed nuts, ground hard-boiled eggs or a handful of Muscat raisins.

SUGGESTED ACCOMPANIMENTS

Steamed or fried rice — Noodles — Do not forget the traditional Chutney served separately.

Chicken Gumbo

INGREDIENTS

5 chicken breasts, boned
   and cut in chunks
2 tablespoons vegetable oil
1 large onion, finely minced
1 green pepper, chopped "julienne"
5 ripe tomatoes; peeled, seeded
   and mashed or
   1 can (20 oz.) tomatoes
1 can (24 oz.) okra or
   1 box frozen okra, thawed
   and sliced

SERVINGS
5

PREPARATION
25 minutes

SOAKING TIME OF CLAY BAKER
10 minutes

BAKING TIME
350° F. 1½ hours

SEASONINGS
1 teaspoon nutmeg
1 teaspoon marjoram
salt and pepper to taste

DIRECTIONS

Oil bottom of baker — Add pieces of chicken — Put on top: onions, green pepper, tomatoes, okras — Sprinkle with seasoning — Close and bake.

SUGGESTED ACCOMPANIMENTS

Steamed rice — A chicory salad with roquefort vinaigrette goes well — This colourful dish does not require more vegetables.

Coq au Vin

INGREDIENTS
1 5 pound chicken cut in serving pieces
3 strips bacon (lean), cut fine
12 small onions
1 clove garlic, crushed
1 quart mushrooms, minced
1½ cups red wine
2 tablespoons cognac

SERVINGS
4

PREPARATION
25 minutes

SOAKING TIME OF CLAY BAKER
10 minutes

BAKING TIME
275° F. 2½ hours

SEASONINGS
2 bay leaves, crushed
2 parsley sprigs
1 teaspoon thyme
salt and pepper to taste

DIRECTIONS
Line clay baker with bacon — Add pieces of chicken — Sprinkle with garlic and seasoning — Moisten with wine and cognac — Close and bake two hours — Add mushrooms and onions one-half hour before end of baking time.

SUGGESTED ACCOMPANIMENTS
Parslied potatoes, rice or noodles — Green sweet peas — Celeriac salad "en vinaigrette".

Italian Stuffed Liver

INGREDIENTS

6 large slices of veal liver,
thinly cut

1 onion, finely chopped

STUFFING

½ pound minced veal
liver trimmings, finely
minced

1 clove garlic, mashed

2 pinches savory

salt and pepper

1 egg white

1 pat of butter on each slice
of meat

SERVINGS
4 or more

PREPARATION
25 minutes

SOAKING TIME OF CLAY BAKER
15 minutes

BAKING TIME
350° F. 1 hour

SEASONINGS
4 fennel leaves, finely
chopped

salt and pepper to taste

DIRECTIONS

Mix thoroughly minced veal, trimmings, savory, garlic, seasoning and egg white — Spread the stuffing on slices — Roll into cigar shapes and skewer each roll — Put pats of butter on each — Line clay baker with onion and fennel — Arrange rows diagonally — Close and bake — Sprinkle with fresh parsley or chives before serving.

SUGGESTED ACCOMPANIMENTS

Spaghetti with tomato sauce topped with grated parmesan or emmenthal cheese — Italian style green salad.

Stuffed Veal Shoulder

INGREDIENTS

3 pounds rolled shoulder of veal
½ pound ground ham
4 shallots with greens, chopped
1 parsley sprig, chopped
½ cup bread crumbs moistened in milk and squeezed dry
1 egg, lightly beaten
juice of ½ lemon
2 tablespoons dry white wine or white vermouth

SERVINGS
6

PREPARATION
35 minutes

SOAKING TIME OF CLAY BAKER
10 minutes

BAKING TIME
300° F. 2½ hours

SEASONINGS
2 teaspoons sage
1 teaspoon allspice
salt and pepper to taste

DIRECTIONS

In a large bowl blend the following stuffing with wet hands: ground ham, shallots, parsley, bread, egg, lemon juice, sage, spices, salt and pepper — Unroll shoulder and take off as much fat as possible — Spread stuffing evenly — Roll and tie but not too tightly — Moisten with wine — Close and bake.

SUGGESTED ACCOMPANIMENTS

Fresh new vegetables in season or potatoes "savoyard" — If you wish to be exotic: baked banana "à la Martiniquaise" — Chicory salad with apples and a sour cream dressing.

NOTE — Ask your butcher to bone the meat, thus making your work easier when stuffing it. A flat cut of boned breast may also be stuffed.

Veal Cutlets with Orange Sauce

INGREDIENTS
8 veal scallops ½ inch thick
1 onion, finely diced
juice of 1 orange
rind of 1 orange, grated
½ cup chicken broth
2 tablespoons sherry
1 orange, peeled and sliced
(to garnish)

SERVINGS
4

PREPARATION
15 minutes

SOAKING TIME OF CLAY BAKER
10 minutes

BAKING TIME
350° F. 1 hour

SEASONINGS
1 teaspoon dry mustard
1 teaspoon ginger
salt and pepper

DIRECTIONS
Put onion in clay baker — Add scallops on top — Sprinkle with orange peel and juice — Season — Moisten with sherry — Close and bake — Garnish with thinly sliced peeled orange just before serving.

SUGGESTED ACCOMPANIMENTS
Spinach noodles or sweet potatoes — Boston lettuce or iceberg lettuce.

Veal with Wood Sorrel

INGREDIENTS
8 or more veal chops cut thick
½ pound sorrel
4 strips bacon
2 carrots, sliced
2 onions, minced
1 cup good stock (veal or chicken broth)
2 tablespoons white vermouth

SERVINGS
4

PREPARATION
15 minutes

SOAKING TIME OF CLAY BAKER
10 minutes

BAKING TIME
350° F. 1 hour

SEASONINGS
2 teaspoons savory
salt and pepper to taste

DIRECTIONS
Make a deep bed of wood sorrel — Add pieces of meat and seasoning — Put bacon on top of chops — Spread onions and carrots — Moisten with broth and vermouth — Season a last time — Close and bake.

SUGGESTED ACCOMPANIMENTS
Large spinach noodles moistened with the juice from the casserole, sprinkled with paprika and poppy seeds — Carrots.

NOTE — Sorrel is an abundant country plant that grows mostly in sunny acid soil. It is described as a sour-leafed version of spinach. If you cannot find sorrel, spinach may be substituted, sprinkled with the juice of one lemon. A spinach and sorrel combination is an elegant dish.

Veal Tongue Michel

INGREDIENTS
5 small fresh tongues
1 onion, minced
4 carrots, sliced
1 celery stalk with leaves, chopped
juice of 1 lemon
2 cups or more of water

SERVINGS
6

PREPARATION
20 minutes

SOAKING TIME OF CLAY BAKER
10 minutes

BAKING TIME
300° F. 2 hours

SEASONINGS
4 whole cloves
2 bay leaves
1 teaspoon cardamom
salt and pepper to taste

DIRECTIONS
Scrub tongues with warm water to clean well — Place on bottom of clay baker: onions, carrots, celery — Put tongues on this bed — Dot with cloves, crushed bay leaves, seasoning — Cover with water — Close and bake — When tongues are well cooked, drain and dip in cold water; slit the skin and peel it off — Cut off the bone and gristle at the thick end.

SUGGESTED ACCOMPANIMENTS
Mousseline potatoes, carrots — Sauce made with dried currants (2 cups currants, 1 cup water, ½ cup brown sugar, lemon juice, nutmeg and allspice) — Cook slowly to a syrup — If you like it spicy, add 1 tablespoon wine vinegar, a dash of red and white pepper to taste — Finish with a watercress salad "en vinaigrette".

Veal Sirloin Roast

INGREDIENTS

3½ to 4 pound veal sirloin
  roast
4 strips bacon
2 parsley sprigs
3 carrots, sliced
3 onions, minced
juice of ½ lemon
½ cup fresh chopped parsley

SERVINGS
5

PREPARATION
20 minutes

SOAKING TIME OF CLAY BAKER
10 minutes

BAKING TIME
350° F. 2½ hours

SEASONINGS
1 teaspoon thyme
2 bay leaves
salt and pepper to
  taste

DIRECTIONS

Arrange parsley, carrots, onions in clay baker — Add roast — Cover with bacon strips — Moisten with lemon juice — Add seasoning — Close and bake — Dot with fresh parsley just before serving.

SUGGESTED ACCOMPANIMENTS

Potatoes "Duchesse" — Green beans with toasted slivered almonds — Boston lettuce with caper sauce. This menu makes a grand dinner.

Veal Stew

INGREDIENTS

5 veal hind shanks, cut into crosswise pieces 1½ or 2 inches thick

2 onions, chopped

2 cloves garlic, crushed

1 cup dry white wine (or dry cider)

5 large ripe tomatoes (in season); peeled, seeded mashed or

1 can (20 oz.) pear tomatoes, (remove seeds and water)

1 tablespoon tomato paste diluted in the wine or cider

1 orange rind, grated

SERVINGS
4 or more

PREPARATION
20 minutes

SOAKING TIME OF CLAY BAKER
10 minutes

BAKING TIME
300° F. 3 hours

SEASONINGS
1 teaspoon basil

1 teaspoon rosemary

salt

cayenne pepper to taste

DIRECTIONS

Season shanks generously on all sides — Put onions and garlic in clay baker first, then meat — Pour in wine or cider — Add tomatoes — Season well — Sprinkle with orange rind — Close and bake.

SUGGESTED ACCOMPANIMENTS

Saffron rice (rice cooked in chicken broth with a pinch of saffron) — Or spaghetti — Cauliflower — Spinach salad with lemon.

Curried Veal

INGREDIENTS
2½ pounds boned veal (breast, shoulder or shank), cut in 2 inch pieces
1 onion, minced
3 apples, pared and cored
½ cup bouillon (veal or chicken)
½ cup white wine
1 lemon, pressed

SERVINGS
5

PREPARATION
25 minutes

SOAKING TIME OF CLAY BAKER
15 minutes

BAKING TIME
350° F. 1½ hours

SEASONINGS
1 tablespoon hot curry powder
1 pinch of ginger or 1 teaspoon grated fresh ginger
salt
cayenne pepper to taste

DIRECTIONS
Trim all excess fat from meat — Put onions and apples in clay baker — Add meat — Moisten with wine, bouillon and lemon juice — Season evenly (as hot as you like it) — Close and bake.

SUGGESTED ACCOMPANIMENTS
Boiled rice — Braised cauliflower with parmesan cheese — Escarole salad garnished with small beets or endives garnished with capers in a cream dressing. You may also simply serve with steamed rice and a plate of chutney.

Sweetbreads with Raisins

INGREDIENTS

2 pounds sweetbreads
4 strips bacon
2 parsley sprigs, chopped
2 chervil sprigs, chopped
2 onions, finely chopped
2 carrots, sliced
½ cup pure grape juice
¼ cup bouillon (veal or chicken)
2 tablespoons sherry (dry)
1 cup Muscat raisins (white)
juice of ½ lemon

SERVINGS
4

PREPARATION
30 minutes

SOAKING TIME OF CLAY BAKER
10 minutes

BAKING TIME
350° F. 1 hour

SEASONINGS
2 bay leaves
1 teaspoon allspice
salt and pepper to taste

DIRECTIONS

Let sweetbreads soak in cold water overnight if possible, or at least six hours to extract clogged blood — Slip off the fine membrane with your fingers and cut out the dark veins and thick membrane — Place bacon on bottom of the clay baker — Make a bed of parsley, chervil, onions, carrots — Finish with sweetbread moistened with grape, lemon juices and sherry — Season — Close and bake — Add Muscat raisins half-hour before the end of baking time.

SUGGESTED ACCOMPANIMENTS

Creole rice or curried rice — Fiddlehead greens or asparagus — Scraped carrots with lemon and oil dressing.

Veal with Eggplant

INGREDIENTS

2 pounds veal shoulder or breast cut in thin strips

1 tablespoon oil

2 parsley sprigs, chopped

2 onions, minced

1 medium-sized eggplant, pared and diced

½ cup white wine (or dry cider)

juice of ½ lemon

2 cloves garlic, crushed

4 fresh tomatoes (in season), peeled, crushed and seeded or 1 can (20 oz.) stewed tomatoes

SERVINGS

4 or more

PREPARATION

30 minutes

SOAKING TIME OF CLAY BAKER

10 minutes

BAKING TIME

350° F. 1½ hours

SEASONINGS

1 teaspoon allspice

1 teaspoon tarragon

salt and pepper to taste

DIRECTIONS

Let pared and diced eggplant stand covered with coarse salt 30 minutes — Rinse vigorously under cold running water — Pat dry — Oil bottom of clay baker — Add in layers: veal, parsley, onions, eggplant — Moisten with wine or cider and lemon — Finish with tomatoes, garlic, more herbs and seasoning — Close and bake.

SUGGESTED ACCOMPANIMENTS

Garlic spaghetti — Braised fennel or asparagus en vinaigrette in season.

Braised Veal with Tomatoes

INGREDIENTS

8 veal cutlets cut thick
1 tablespoon oil
2 tablespoons grated parmesan
  cheese
1 tablespoon tomato ketchup
1 tablespoon drained horseradish
1 clove garlic, crushed
½ lemon, squeezed
2 or more quartered tomatoes
  in season, or
  1 can Italian tomatoes,
  seeded, without juice (to garnish)

SERVINGS
4

PREPARATION
25 minutes

SOAKING TIME OF CLAY BAKER
10 minutes

BAKING TIME
350° F. 1 hour

SEASONINGS
1 teaspoon dry mustard
1 tablespoon chervil
1 tablespoon parsley
salt and pepper to taste

DIRECTIONS

Rub cutlets with mustard — Put on each: cheese, ketchup, horseradish, garlic, herbs, seasoning and a touch of lemon — Fold in half and pin with one or two toothpicks — Oil bottom of clay baker — Lay cutlets in rows — Season again — Close and bake — 20 minutes before serving, arrange tomatoes on top of cutlets — Return to oven for remainder of cooking time — If available (in season), add minced chervil, chives to enhance the colouring of your dish just before bringing in to the table.

SUGGESTED ACCOMPANIMENTS

Lima beans with butter or beans Spanish style — Macaroni — Zucchini or eggplant are also good — A green salad. All of these complement the meal.

Veal Marengo

INGREDIENTS

2½ pounds veal (front shank, shoulder, neck, round or rump)

1 tablespoon oil

2 parsley sprigs, chopped

2 onions, finely chopped

1 clove garlic, crushed

½ cup dry white wine

juice of ½ lemon

2 tablespoons tomato paste

1 can small whole mushrooms

24 pitted green olives

SERVINGS
5

PREPARATION
25 minutes

SOAKING TIME OF CLAY BAKER
10 minutes

BAKING TIME
350° F. 1½ hours

SEASONINGS
2 bay leaves
2 teaspoons tarragon
salt and pepper to taste

DIRECTIONS

Oil bottom of clay baker — Add parsley, onions, meat and garlic — Moisten with wine in which you have diluted tomato paste — Sprinkle with herbs, a dash of lemon, salt and pepper — Close and bake one hour — Remove clay baker — Add mushrooms and olives — Bake another half-hour.

SUGGESTED ACCOMPANIMENTS

Large egg noodles with garlic, butter and poppy seeds — Carrots and celery, garnished with ripe olives.

INDEX

○ ○ ○ ○

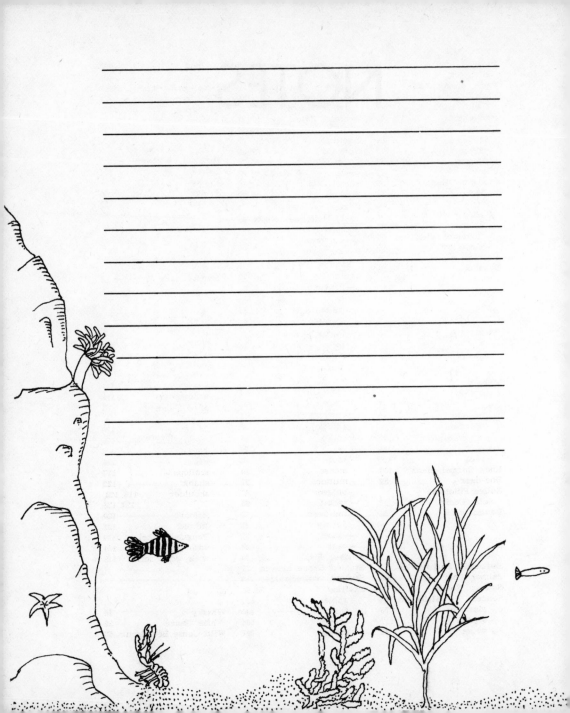

NOTES

_____

_____

o_____

o_____

_____

_____

o_____

o_____

o_____

_____

o_____

_____

_____

_____

_____

_____

_____

_____

_____

_____

_____

_____

_____

_____

_____

_____

_____

_____